IT'S ABOUT TIME

A Practical Guide to Managing Your Most Important Resource

Stewart L. Stokes, Jr.

CBI CBI Publishing Company, Inc.
51 Sleeper Street
Boston, Massachusetts 02210

Library of Congress Cataloging in Publication Data

Stokes, Stewart L., 1935–
  It's about time.

  Bibliography: p.
  1. Time management.   I. Title.
HD38.S729   646.7   81-21790
ISBN 0-8436-0878-1   AACR2

Printed in the United States of America.

Printing (*last digit*): 9 8 7 6 5 4 3 2 1

Contents

Preface

What motivated you to pick up this book? What is causing you to flip through it, to glance at the chapter headings, to quickly review some of the exercises and checklists, to begin to read this page? Is the reason a vague but disturbing feeling of not having control over your time? Or did your most recent performance review indicate that you needed to pay more attention to deadlines? Perhaps you are gripped by the familiar feeling of going in too many directions at once. On the other hand, the reverse may be true: you're in the clutches of "paralysis of analysis" and can't seem to decide in which direction to turn. Is it because you have recently accepted new responsibilities that will add to your pressures? Or, you may be trying to divest yourself of tasks that you feel you have outgrown. Perhaps you're just plain curious!

Whatever your reason, I believe that this book, the workshop exercises, and the accompanying tape will help you deal constructively with the many and often conflicting time pressures you experience. You're not alone when you wonder how you are going to finish this week's work, let alone begin on next week's assignments. You're not the first person—nor will you be the last—who ever asked, "Why am I doing all this, anyway? What sense does it make? What am I contributing?"

This book and these tapes are designed to be used by people in all walks of life, in a variety of situations. The material will be helpful to:

- supervisors and managers with technical backgrounds
- new supervisors and managers in complex organizations
- administrators in nonprofit organizations
- managers in smaller companies
- staff specialists who are "knowledge workers" and who report to line managers
- people preparing to enter—or re-enter—the job market
- people in mid-career who contemplate—or who are faced with—a change of job direction.

Whatever your situation, you should find something of value by reading these pages, listening to the tape, and working on the exercises.

A word of caution, however: you will not find specific answers to your time management problems within these pages. It would be presumptuous of me to think that I could present you with easy answers to problem situations that are often highly personal, ambiguous in nature, and rooted in complex organizational situations. The answers that will work for you lie within yourself, and *you* must take responsibility for working them out.

You will find, however, an approach, a pattern, a model that will be useful as you make the many day-to-day decisions about what it is you want to accomplish, when you want to accomplish it, and how you want to get it done. To experience this book will be to begin a journey that I hope will continue throughout your life: a journey characterized by *proactive planning* for the events, decisions, and results that are important to you. In a nutshell, I want to encourage *proactive* instead of *reactive* behavior.

It's only natural that some readers will expect an "armchair adventure" and will anticipate answers that will sweep away their time management problems. To provide "cookbook" or "band-aid" cure-alls is not my objective—although I will liberally sprinkle time control tips throughout this book. My objective is to raise questions about your use of the most precious and valuable resource you possess—your time and your life. The final decisions are up to you. How you make those decisions is the topic of this book and the accompanying tape; it is the thread running throughout the material.

A bibliography of books about time management appears later in this book. The list is not meant to be complete. New material is being developed constantly. The list is meant to be representative of various points of view, however, and I recommend all of the books to you.

Now, if your time and your life are of interest to you, read on!

CHAPTER ONE

Time: Attributes of It, Attitudes Toward It

ASSUMPTIONS ABOUT YOU

There are six assumptions that I have made about the readers and users of this material. They are assumptions about you, your present situation, and your attitudes toward time. These assumptions have proven to be accurate when applied to many of the people with whom I have worked in my time management seminars.

Here they are. I suggest you check off the statements that apply most to you. We'll say more about them later on.

1. *You are a busy person,* very much involved with your life, your career—or at least a job.
2. *You seem to have more "things" to do than time in which to do them.* You sometimes feel as if you're going in several different directions at once.
3. *You do not have extensive blocks of time* to sit down and devote to this material, to do the exercises, and listen to the tape.

4. *You are concerned about how you are using your time* and wonder whether you're devoting the proper amount of time and energy to the "right things."

5. *You sometimes wonder if you're the only one around who is experiencing time pressures* and who is frustrated occasionally by the many competing demands on your life.

6. *You would like to apply immediately some of what we discuss* to your own life, job, and career.

USING THIS MATERIAL

If you checked five or six of the above statements, congratulations! You are not only in good company, you stand an excellent chance of benefiting greatly from this material. Most of us feel busy and seem to have more work to do than time in which to do it. Few of us are blessed with large chunks of free time. Almost all of us are concerned about our time (or lack of it) and wonder if we're the only people around with such "problems." We say over and over again that we would like to do something—*anything*—about our situations.

I have written this book and the accompanying tape with the time control needs of the busy person in mind. The material is designed to be an active learning experience. You can use the material as an individual or in a group, at home or in the office, commuting by car or in an airplane. You can read the book from cover to cover, not stopping to do any of the exercises, or you can pause as you go along, creating a workshop environment by participating in the experiences and reflecting on the results. You will find the material easy to use in your spare time, at home, or in a "brown bag" lunch-time seminar around someone's desk at the office. A husband and wife can work together, or each may work singly—but perhaps comparing results as they go along!

I have designed this material as a "conversation." As I am writing it, I am visualizing you listening to me through these pages. My time management workshops are not "armchair adventures," and this material is developed to be used over and over again. If you were to participate in one of my workshops, I would ask you to do more than listen and take notes. I would expect you to be involved in the activities, drawing on your own aspirations, your own needs, and your own objectives. I will urge you to do the same as you go through this workbook. Think of this as a personal seminar in time management, developed exclusively for you!

You will note the workshop pages throughout the book. If you wish you may reproduce and re-use them. The audio tape supplements the written material and is meant to be used as a refresher, and when working with a book is not practical. An important benefit of this material is that you don't need all day or an extensive block of hours to make progress. A few minutes at a time is all that is necessary—so let's begin.

ATTRIBUTES OF TIME

Time is a resource. As a resource it is often overlooked and mismanaged, but it is nevertheless one of the important resources we have at our disposal. When we think of resources, most of us think about:

- tangible items, including plant, equipment, machinery, fixtures, and furniture
- money and assets that can be converted into cash
- people and their knowledge, skills, and abilities
- information that can be used to advantage by our organizations and ourselves.

More and more, however, we are coming to realize that time is the most valuable resource of all. Many of us sense this as we grow older. "The days hurry by," in the words of a popular song of not so long ago. As they "hurry by" for us as individuals, we come to realize that our days are limited, and we need to use them for the things that are most important to us, to our families, to those we love and care about. As we begin to think in these terms, we begin to formulate objectives that we will use as we become *proactive* in our time management.

You and I have all the time there is, twenty-four hours a day, each and every day, for the rest of our lives. The use we make of this precious resource will often mean the difference between success or mediocrity, self-fulfillment or vague uneasiness, profit or loss, growth or the status quo. The curious paradox for many of us is that while we have all the time there is, we say we never have enough. We complain about not having enough time to attend this meeting or that program, to do this project or that activity, to read this book or see that movie. We say, "I don't have enough time to exercise" or "I wish I had time to learn a foreign language . . . or play the piano . . . or take a vacation . . . or whatever." Many of our lives are filled with promises and resolutions to ourselves, and countless laments of "I wish. . . ."

Let's be honest. What we're really saying when we complain about not having enough time to do all we say we want to do is that the "doing" is just not a priority for us. We feel a bit guilty, perhaps, and we attempt to rationalize this vague guilt feeling by telling all who will listen that "I really wanted to do that, but I just didn't have the time." Think back to the most recent occasion when you said you wanted to do something. How much did you really want to do it? How important was the "doing" to you? Why was it important? Did you honestly want to do it, or were you feeling pressured into it? Were you going to do it for the wrong reasons?

TIME MANAGEMENT IS PRIORITY MANAGEMENT

Time management and time control are really *priority* management and *priority* control. The most difficult but important word to learn is "no." We will never learn to manage our time and our lives effectively until we learn how to say "yes" to some activities, projects, and goals, and "no" to others.

Let's stop for a moment and accomplish two important tasks. First, examine your attitudes about time and your use of it as a resource. Second, list several skills, behaviors, tasks, projects, responsibilities, etc. that you feel are important for you to change and improve. Also, begin thinking about why it is important that you change and improve them. This will, I hope, begin to encourage you to think about what is really significant to you and what you should be using your time to accomplish.

ATTITUDES ARE CLUES

A few words about attitudes may be helpful. Attitudes are clues. The attitudes we express about conditions or situations in our lives are some of the most important indicators we have to explain our behavior toward those conditions or situations. Our behaviors are reflections of our attitudes and values. Our attitudes about time, for instance, will give us important clues as to the reasons behind our use—or misuse—of time. We can often obtain short-term behavior shifts in our use of time by following some of the popular "tips for time management" so prevalent in business literature today. However, significant changes and results in the way we manage time as a resource will come about only as we develop new attitudes and values about this resource and the impact it has on our lives, relationships, and careers.

Please complete Worksheet One and reveal some insights into your own attitudes about time. Don't try to fool yourself. Be honest. There are no right or wrong responses. There is no "best" answer. The important thing is to learn more about how you feel concerning the time in your life. You can do this more effectively by thinking, writing, and talking about it than you can by merely reading about it.

Turn to Worksheet One. It's entitled, "Conversation Starters: With Myself and Others." You are to write one or more sentences in completion of each set of key words. For instance, you might write in response to item number one, "Yesterday I overslept, was late for work, missed an important meeting, and fell even more behind on an important assignment." Or, in response to item seven, "When I think about time I think of all the things I never did and I get frustrated. So I don't think about it anymore." Go ahead now; begin.

COMPLETE WORKSHEET ONE

Conversation Starters: With Myself and Others

WORKSHEET ONE

Conversation Starters: With Myself and Others

1. Yesterday I . . .

2. So far this week . . .

3. My life is . . .

4. My family . . .

5. Next month I . . .

6. My career is . . .

7. When I think about time I . . .

8. The most important thing . . .

9. My biggest regret is . . .

10. Last year . . .

11. My spouse . . .

12. People who know me best suggest . . .

13. My children . . .

14. I never . . .

15. What I really want is . . .

16. Next time I will . . .

17. If I had to do it over I . . .

18. What I really want to change is . . .

19. Tomorrow . . .

20. By the end of this year I will have . . .

21. My job . . .

22. I will improve myself by . . .

23. My boss . . .

24. My performance on the job . . .

25. I often feel . . .

RESPONSES AND THEIR SIGNIFICANCE

Now, if you are working alone, review your responses and think carefully and thoughtfully about them. Reflect on the "why" behind each statement. For instance, why did you oversleep, miss that meeting, and fall farther behind? (Question Number One). Had you not used your time to prepare for the meeting and were you trying to avoid unpleasant consequences? Were you resenting the intrusion of another "worthless meeting" into an already overcrowded schedule? Or were you just plain tired from having worked long hours of overtime attempting to catch up on that "important assignment?"

What are you telling yourself about your use of time? What attitudes are revealed? What behaviors follow? What are you learning about yourself? What attitudes and behaviors might you want to change? If you are working with others, compare your responses and discuss them. Discuss "why" you respond as you do. Look behind your responses. What is the "music" behind the words? Why do you react as you do? What are you telling yourself and others about the most important resource in your life?

Let's suppose that, in response to item fourteen, you wrote, "I never . . . have enough time to do all the things I want to do; as a result, nothing gets done." What are you really saying? What is going on here? Many people respond in that way. What they may be revealing is that they have failed to adequately sort out their priorities and, as a result, they are unable to focus their efforts and energies on the tasks, projects, and activities that will contribute most to their accomplishing worthwhile objectives. These people have not really come to grips with what is important to them in their daily lives. Until they do this—and monitor continually their changing priorities—all the time management tips in the world will make little difference in the long run.

People of different ages will often express varying attitudes about time. So will people with different motivational drives. It's important that we have these insights, for they are often clues to more effective time control on the job and in everyday organizational life. For instance, the view of time may be quite different for an individual nearing retirement than it is for a younger person who has just received his or her first promotion. As we grow older, time does seem to slip away from us. Time seems to move faster and faster; in fact, it has been suggested that this sensation stems from a slowing down of chemical activity in the body as it ages.[1]

Also, an achievement-oriented individual who is motivated by an inner drive to accomplish assignments and achieve results "in a hurry" will view time and its use in quite a different manner from the person who places much value in cultivating warm feelings of acceptance and respect from his or her co-workers. Line managers are often highly results-oriented; they are, of necessity, task-focused and super-sensitive to accomplishing results "here and now." This sometimes gets in the way of good delegation and causes them to work longer hours than might otherwise be necessary. Many, however, would have it no other way.

Staff specialists tend to be more process-oriented than their line manager colleagues. They understand the need for results accomplishment but recognize the often time-consuming process that must be worked through in order to enable the organization to function smoothly. Indeed, the continuing tension between task accomplishment and process sensitivity is at the root of many time management conflicts in organizational life.

The value of sharing and comparing attitudes is not so much in what particular points of view may be revealed as it is in recognizing the fact that our actions and use of time will reflect the attitudes we have about time. The more insight we develop into the points of view others have, the better we will be able to work with—and for—them.

TIME CONTROL IS SELF-CONTROL

To manage our time means to manage ourselves. Time control is self-control. One of the reasons many of us find the management of time so frustrating is because it means we need to manage *ourselves* more effectively. The little comic strip character was right: "We have met the enemy and he is us." Many of us manage others more easily and effectively than we manage ourselves. We do things that we ought not to do and we leave undone the things that we should have done. We can be our own best friends *and* our own worst enemies.

---

1. Webber, Ross A. *Time and Management* New York: Van Nostrand Reinhold Company, 1972.

I mentioned earlier that a person's attitudes underlie his or her behavior. Your actions and use of time, then, reflect the attitudes you have about time. In order for you to change the way you live and change the way you use your time, you must *want* to change; you must *want* to alter your behavior. All the books and all the coursework in the world will make little difference if the desire to alter your priorities is absent. Until you want to change, little will happen. When you want to change, all things are possible.

As a first step in changing your use of time, you were asked to examine your attitudes about time by completing a group of "conversation starters." I suggested you discuss your responses and the reasons for them with others. Now, as a second step I suggest you take a look toward your own "time horizon" and begin to focus on elements in your life and career that you wish to change and improve. Think in terms of:

- *knowledge and understanding*
  (What would you like to know more about and understand better?)
- *skills and behaviors*
  (What would you like to be able to do more effectively?)
- *relationships and situations*
  (What would you like to improve? With whom? What would you like to do differently?)
- *tasks and projects*
  (What would you like to undertake? Move along more swiftly? Complete?)
- *responsibilities*
  (What would you like more of? What would you like to shift to another department, to someone else?)
- *hobbies and leisure-time pursuits*
  (What new activity would you like to learn more about? Do more frequently? Begin?)

In other words, think about whatever in your life you feel would benefit from change and improvement.

A FOUR-STEP PATTERN FOR CHANGE AND IMPROVEMENT

Worksheet Two entitled, "Time Changes," outlines a four-step pattern for thinking about change. It suggests we first decide what it is we wish to change and improve. After we make this decision, we focus on the outcome we want, or the objective we want to achieve. Thirdly, we establish the reason or reasons we wish to make the change and improvement and finally, we decide upon our target date for completion of the change.

By going through this process we begin to set behavioral objectives for ourselves. Behavioral objectives are action-oriented; that is, they mean that some action on our part will be required in order to complete them in a satisfactory manner. We've already established that attitudes underlie behavior; it's therefore important for us to be explicit with regard to the reasons we wish to undertake a particular change or improvement project. Unless we have a positive attitude about the need for change and then commit ourselves to the process, little of real significance will happen.

Look now at Worksheet Two, "Time Changes." It consists, first, of a series of four statements relating to change-oriented objectives. The statements are followed by two examples of common business-oriented change and improvement. You may have vowed to improve your knowledge, understanding, and skill in both areas yourself! One change relates to improving reading speed and comprehension. The other relates to improving the understanding of financial statement ratio analysis; the skill to apply key ratios to one's own corporate financial statements, and finally, the ability to discuss the company's financial position with a key financial officer.

The two examples are followed by space in which you should develop five statements of change and improvement that are important to you. I suggest you stop and develop at least three before proceeding further. You may want to return to them later.

COMPLETE WORKSHEET TWO

Time Changes

WORKSHEET TWO

Time Changes

1.   I wish to change and improve:

2.   The outcome I want is:

3.   The reason I wish to change is:

4.   My target date is:

Example number one:

1.   I wish to change and improve: My reading speed and comprehension.
2.   The outcome I want is: To read business reports at x words per minute and increase my comprehension by n percent; To read leisure-time reading at y words per minute and increase comprehension by q percent.
3.   The reason I wish to change is: I'm tired of staying late at the office finishing required reading and never having time to complete popular novels others are enjoying.
4.   My target date is: Three months from today.

Example number two:

1.   I wish to change and improve: My understanding of how to read corporate financial statements.
2.   The outcome I want is: To know and understand at least six key ratios pertaining to the analysis of financial statements; to be able to apply these ratios to my own company's financial statement; to be able to talk intelligently with my financial vice-president about our company's financial position.
3.   The reason I wish to change is: Because the younger managers now working for me all know more than I do about "numbers crunching," and I'm embarrassed about my lack of understanding of financial concerns.
4.   My target date is: By the end of next week.

1. I wish to change and improve:

2. The outcome I want is:

3. The reason I wish to change is:

4. My target date is:

---

1. I wish to change and improve:

2. The outcome I want is:

3. The reason I wish to change is:

4. My target date is:

---

1. I wish to change and improve:

2. The outcome I want is:

3. The reason I wish to change is:

4. My target date is:

WORKSHEET TWO (continued)

1. I wish to change and improve:

2. The outcome I want is:

3. The reason I wish to change is:

4. My target date is:

---

1. I wish to change and improve:

2. The outcome I want is:

3. The reason I wish to change is:

4. My target date is:

---

1. I wish to change and improve:

2. The outcome I want is:

3. The reason I wish to change is:

4. My target date is:

By now you are probably beginning to appreciate more why we say that time is truly one of our most important resources and assets. Many people fail to think of it in these terms. Because of the failure to realize the significance of the time resource, they waste it and use it for low-priority items, tasks, and projects, and wonder why they always feel "behind."

An asset is defined as, "A useful or valuable quality or thing . . . any possession on hand . . . and available for use; actual and potential wealth."[2] A common synonym is "resource." Time certainly qualifies as an asset and a resource. It is probably our most overlooked and underrated resource, however. It is also the key resource that successful managers have at their disposal for turning situations and opportunities into "actual or potential wealth" for their organizations and themselves. And every manager, regardless of level in the organization and charter of expectations in the job description, bears responsibility for contributing to the present and future wealth of the organization. This "bottom line" responsibility must be accepted and acted upon. It is the life-blood of a company, and the first priority of every business organization must be self-perpetuation

Time, as an asset and a resource, is every bit as important as plant and equipment, money, people, and information. We don't usually think of it as such and that's why most of us fail to use it wisely. If you doubt this statement, go and speak with a colleague who has just missed an important deadline, or one whose latest personnel evaluation revealed that, in the opinion of senior management, he or she is "lacking in effectiveness due to spending too much time on low-priority, low-payoff activities" and not enough time on "high-priority projects that will contribute significantly to the achievement of corporate objectives." All the tangible assets, money, and people in the world will fail to bring back the time that could have been focused on the high-payoff priority objectives. So many of us lack the self-discipline necessary to, first of all, determine what our priority objectives are; then to figure out how we're going to achieve them; and finally, to monitor and fine-tune our expenditure of time so that it is applied to what I call our "key areas for concentration."

---

2. William Morris, ed. *The American Heritage Dictionary of the English Language.* Boston: American Heritage Publishing Co., Inc., and Houghton Mifflin Publishing Co., 1975.

These "key areas" are the critical few tasks, items, and elements that—on any job or assignment—will produce most of the results we want. It's been demonstrated statistically that we will get 80 percent of our results, in terms of "output," from 20 percent of the above-mentioned tasks, items, and elements, or "input." Statistically, in any given group, the significant items in terms of value will normally constitute a relatively small proportion of total items in the group. Eighty percent of the value will come from 20 percent of the items. As it is applied to effective time control, I call this the principle of "focused accountability."

As I discussed earlier in this chapter, time is the scarcest resource of all. No matter how much we say we need "extra time" to complete a certain project, task, or assignment, we cannot borrow or manufacture more of it. We cannot buy it and we certainly cannot set it aside or stockpile it for a "rainy day." Each and every one of us has all the time there is, yet most of us say we don't have enough. Again, what we're really saying when we exclaim "I just don't have enough time to do that," is that the "doing" of that project is just not a priority for us at that particular moment.

Time is a unique resource, in that it is the measure we use for the passing of our lives. As such it often becomes a confusing resource. It is, at the same moment, an opportunity and a tyrant. You feel you "should be" doing one thing but that you "ought to be" doing another. As a result, you often do neither, and wind up frustrated and upset. Unfortunately, there are no easy answers to these often conflicting and troubling situations, but you must move forward, making your decisions about employing your time resource as best you can. The thesis of this book is that you can employ time best when you have a clear understanding of the objectives you wish to achieve, both in terms of your personal life and your career.

KEY WORDS IN TIME MANAGEMENT

As we conclude this first chapter, I would like to suggest several key words as having special significance for time management and time control. If you continually hold these words and their meanings in mind, you will never be far from effective time management. These words, and their significance for managing time, are as follows:

Objectives: What do you wish to accomplish, when, and why?

Priorities: From your multitude of competing activities, which are most important to you in terms of the objectives you wish to accomplish? What are your priority activities and priority objectives?

Key areas for concentration: What are the relatively few activities or action steps that will contribute the most to accomplishing your objectives? Where must you focus your attention and concentrate your energies? Once you know where, the need to train your sights and manage your time and energy for those areas becomes self-evident, and you will be working toward your objectives.

Discipline: To do all this, you must develop the mental discipline to see it through. To keep resolutions is difficult. To break them is easy. You must overcome yourself and your own inertia. You must get out of your own way and, day-by-day, focus on those elements in your career and your life that will truly make a difference.

Key Points in Chapter One

1. The answers to our time management problems lie within ourselves; there are no "cookbook" solutions. We are all unique, and you must look to yourself, your aspirations and your objectives for the answers that will work for you.

2. Time is an asset, a resource. It is often overlooked and mismanaged; but it is one of the most important resources at your disposal.

3. To manage our time more effectively means to manage ourselves more effectively. Time control is self control. Time management is priority management.

4. A person's behavior is a clue to his or her attitudes toward time and its use. Behavior reflects attitudes and values.

5. When you think and plan for change and improvement, you also must think about why you wish to change and when you wish the change and improvement to be complete.

6. You can employ the time resource most effectively when you have a clear understanding of the objectives you wish to achieve.

7. Key words in time management are:
   - objectives
   - priorities
   - key areas for concentration
   - mental discipline

CHAPTER TWO

Looking at Ourselves

PROJECTIONS

The purpose of this chapter is to encourage you to take an objective look at yourself, the time consumers that most affect you, and the functions, activities, and roles that occupy your time on and off the job. This is important because all of us share at least one fundamental trait when it comes to managing our time resource: we tend to project our time management problems onto others. We spend time and energy blaming others for our time management difficulties. Everyone close to us comes in for his or her share of criticism: our colleagues, our bosses, those who work for us, our children, our spouses, even our customers and friends; no one is immune.

How often have you heard yourself saying:

"If my boss would only: (pick one)
____ leave me alone
____ tell me what (he)(she) expects
____ give me less to do

_____ learn to delegate better
_____ give me a job to do and let me do it
_____ let me have an assistant
_____ schedule fewer meetings
_____ other_____

(insert your criticism here)

I wouldn't have these time management problems.''

or

"If my subordinates would only: (pick one)
_____ work faster
_____ do what I tell them
_____ stop asking so many questions
_____ ask more questions
_____ be more motivated
_____ learn to write better
_____ stay off the phone
_____ other_____

(insert your criticism here)

I wouldn't have these time management problems.''

or

"If my family would only: (pick one)
_____ be more considerate of me
_____ stop doing all these "things"
_____ give me some time to myself
_____ tell me what they want to do
_____ stop signing me up for activities I'm not interested in
_____ learn to read my mind
_____ other_____

(insert your criticism here)

I wouldn't have these time management problems.''

When we're through blaming others, we turn on our surroundings. We blame "the system," our company and the way it's organized, policies and procedures ("too much red tape"), the telephone, meetings, our church, school, and community ("too many activities"). Again, nothing is spared. We look at everyone and everything except ourselves.

How often have you heard yourself saying:

"If (pick one):

_____ we didn't have these rules

_____ this company would get itself organized

_____ the telephone would stop ringing—for just one day!

_____ I didn't have all these meetings to go to

_____ people would stop asking me to do so much

_____ other_____

(insert your criticism here)

I wouldn't have these time management problems."

When we come to grips with the fundamental fact that our use of time is, to a large degree, what we want it to be, we're more than half the way to our goal of making more effective use of this basic resource. When we're ready to stop blaming others and projecting our difficulties onto "the system," we will be ready to start taking the necessary steps to improve the way we manage ourselves. When we decide to look at ourselves in the mirror and recognize that we are the number one cause of our time management frustrations, then we will be in a position to take control of our lives and our careers. As I said in Chapter One, our attitudes underlie our behaviors, and until we change our attitudes toward time usage, all the techniques in the world will have little long-range effect. The fact of the matter is that it's easier to blame your troubles on someone else than it is to look yourself in the eye and begin to work on "number one." Until you do so, however, you're only fooling yourself, and life's too short to waste kidding around!

ALL-TIME TIME CONSUMERS

Let's begin by taking a look at some "All-Time Time Consumers." They are listed on Worksheet Three and have been gathered from a variety of sources including participants in my time management workshops. As you examine this list, ask yourself these six key questions:

1. Which of these all-time time consumers affect me the most?

2. Of those that affect me the most, how am I involved? Am I the cause? Am I part of the problem? In what ways? When? Where? How? With whom? Why?

3. Of those that affect me the most, how are other people involved? Are they the cause? Are they part of the problem? In what ways? When? Where? How? With whom? Why?

4. Of those that affect me the most, which are caused primarily by forces in the job structure or organizational environment? In what ways? When? Where? How? With whom? Why?

5. Of those time consumers that are caused primarily by me, which offer me the best opportunity for change and improvement? In what ways? When? Where? How? With whom?

6. Of those time consumers that are caused primarily by others or by forces in the job structure or organizational environment, which might I do something about . . . to improve . . . to change . . . to influence? In what ways? When? Where? How? With whom?

With these questions in mind, complete Worksheet Three. Review the list of "All-Time Time Consumers" and check those that affect you the most. Ask yourself the six key questions. They are designed to lead to the control and improvement of your most bothersome time consumers. Then turn to Worksheet Four, "Confronting Your Time Consumers." Select a time consumer that you very much want to change and improve upon. Determine a target date for improvement. Then, answer the four questions. Confronting your time consumers in this manner will keep you from projecting them onto others and will enable you to be proactive in seeking solutions for them.

I suggest you refer to Worksheets Three and Four often. Keep track of your time wasters and your progress as you conquer them.

**COMPLETE WORKSHEETS
THREE AND FOUR**

**All-Time Time Consumers
and
Confronting Your Time Consumers**

All-Time Time Consumers

Date_____

Check ( ) those that affect you the most. Then ask yourself the six key questions.

____ Poor listening habits

____ Too much talking

____ Inappropriate conversation

____ Doing instead of managing

____ Difficulty in delegating

____ Involving people who aren't "involved"

____ Failure to find the real problem

____ Premature decision-making or "Paralysis of Analysis"

____ Blame: Fault-finding

____ Jumping to conclusions

____ Fear

____ Time estimates too short

____ Time estimates too long

____ Poor planning

____ No planning

____ Poor organization

____ Overlapping of responsibilities

____ Can't say "no"

____ Doing everything myself

____ Putting it off—procrastination

____ Doing too many things at once

____ Failure to follow through

____ Handling same paperwork over and over again

____ Unclear expectations

____ Lack of information

____ Too much information

____ Misinformation

____ Inconsiderate co-workers

____ Failure to set priorities

____ Failure to get feedback

____ Crisis management

____ Telephone conversations

____ Poorly written communications

____ Meetings

____ Lack of agendas

____ Failure to follow agendas

____ Failure to inform others of your whereabouts

____ Fatigue

____ Junk mail

____ Failure to set policy or procedure to handle routine matters

____ Lack of proper equipment

____ Outdated procedures

____ Low motivation

____ Not knowing what is wanted in delegation

____ Failure to think through when dictating

____ Lack of daily plan

____ Failure to determine "accountabilities"

____ Confusing chain of command

WORKSHEET FOUR

Confronting Your Time Consumers

A time consumer I want to change and improve on is _____

_____

My target date for improvement is_____

1. How am I involved? When? Where? With whom? Why?_____

    _____

    _____

    _____

2. Who else is involved? When? Where? With whom? Why?

    _____

    _____

3. What forces in the organizational environment affect this time consumer? How?
    When? Where? Why? With what effect?_____

    _____

    _____

    _____

4. In what ways might I change and improve on this time consumer? When? Where? With
    whom?_____

    _____

    _____

    _____

YOUR AGENDA FOR SELF-IMPROVEMENT

I suggest you let these time consumers and your responses to the questions serve as part of your agenda for self-improvement. Select target dates for improvement. List ways in which you are involved, when, where, with whom, and why. Determine who else is involved, when, where, with whom, why, and with what effect. Identify the forces in the organizational environment that are affecting your time consumer. Finally, brainstorm ways in which you might change and improve upon this time waster. Let yourself go. Don't be too judgmental too soon. Don't be in a hurry to say "It just won't work." You'll be surprised at the ideas you can think up that will be tentative leads to solving some of your stickiest "all-time time consumers."

For example, let's say you determine that one of the time consumers that affects you the most is "lack of agendas." You spend a great deal of time in conferences and you're disturbed at the amount of time wasted because your boss tends to "wing it" and run his meeting "off the cuff" rather than according to a prepared agenda. You decide that control or elimination of this habit is not realistic because your boss is the one who convenes the meetings. You do feel, however, that you could improve upon the situation. You're not sure how, but anything is an improvement over the status quo. You set a target date for improvement one month from today: four working weeks to promote the habit of making and following an agenda.

You are involved because you attend the meetings. As a matter of fact, you set them up. Your boss decides when one is necessary—often, it seems—and you follow through with the detail work. You book the conference room, memo those who should attend, and tell them what will be discussed.

Others who are involved are first-level supervisors like yourself. They manage other departments similar to yours and you all report to the same person. Meetings are held on the average of three times per week, usually first thing on Monday, Wednesday, and Friday mornings. These are popular times because the get-together enables everyone to communicate about their departments before going their separate ways.

What usually happens, however, is that a 45-minute discussion invariably turns into a two-hour bull session with conversation ranging all the way from pro football results to rumors about the company's competition.

This frustrates you and, depending upon their workload, other supervisors as well. You're sure it bothers the boss but you also know he believes in the open door policy and wouldn't dream of doing anything to stifle conversation. "Got to keep people talking," he's fond of saying. "If they feel they can't talk with you, you're liable to miss out on more important information." You know he's right about the need for open communication. A manager can never have enough information, especially about the competition. But couldn't the boss establish some mutually agreed-upon boundaries around the conversation? Keep it flowing, to be sure, but set some expectations on the direction—and time—it should take?

You decide to brainstorm some ways to do this. However, before approaching the other supervisors with your concern, you decide to come up with several ideas yourself. After thinking about the boss and his needs, the other supervisors and their concerns, and your own time management problems, you decide that the reason the boss doesn't use agendas is not that he is unaware of their value but that he doesn't want to inhibit the flow of information that he feels results from his "free-wheeling" the meetings. You recall a statement he once made to you, that, "I don't like to run a meeting in a lockstep fashion, and a list of numbered items just pens people in."

You finally decide to brainstorm this question: "In what ways might I encourage the boss to try an open-ended, 'keyword' agenda, consisting not of a numbered list of items but of a series of key words and phrases that will mirror the needs of the participants and help keep the conversation on the right track?"

You list numerous suggestions, ranging from the "way out" and inappropriate (bombard the boss with telephone calls from the supervisors begging off attending the meetings) to the mundane (just telling him straight out that he ought to use an agenda). You finally decide on a low-key and appropriate way to call this possibility to his attention. You introduce at the next meeting a discussion of time management problems and suggest that you are going to keep a time log and begin to determine not only where your time is going but how you are falling behind on key jobs as a result of inappropriate time usage. You encourage other supervisors to do the same and ask to discuss the results at a meeting two weeks later.

You proceed to keep your log, adding up the number of hours chewed up in meetings—an average of 6 per week, nearly one full working day! You're sure that when the boss looks at this number and multiplies it by the people usually attending that the result of 42 hours—over one full working week—will stagger him. You will then be in a better position to suggest that a simple "key word" agenda without a rigid series of numbered items will keep the discussion focused on important topics without stifling conversation *or* inhibiting the flow of information. You can predict with reasonable accuracy that a single agenda will save at least 21 person-hours per week by cutting down the time per meeting from two hours to one hour. Put another way, at an average person-cost per hour of $15.00, a simple key-word agenda will save over $300 per week or $15,000 per year! Any manager would be impressed with numbers like these.

THE TWO SIDES TO TIME

It will be obvious by now that there are two sides to the time in our lives: organizational time and personal time. When we refer to organizational time we customarily think of on-the-job time pressures and uses. Conversely, when we refer to personal time, we think of off-the-job time pressures and issues. While those who work and have careers (in the traditional business or professional sense) may be affected more by one side than by the other, all of us experience the tension between time pressures related to our personal and family lives and those related to our jobs, careers, vocations, and volunteer interests.

Which side is of most interest to you? Why? Where do your priorities lie? How much of your personal and family life are you prepared to give up for the sake of career? There are "opportunity costs" attached to your time management decisions. You cannot "have your cake and eat it, too." For instance, those who wish to pursue "fast track" business careers, thereby gaining prestige, promotions, and above-average salaries, must be prepared to give up something in return. Usually this "something" is related to time with family and friends. Not everyone is prepared to make this kind of decision, yet we are all called upon every day to make choices, and we must live with our decisions and their consequences. As far as proactive planning for effective time control is concerned, those who determine what is important to them and act accordingly are usually those who experience the fewest time control pressures and problems.

WHAT IS IMPORTANT TO *YOU?*

Take a moment now and ask yourself which side of your time is of most interest and importance to you. As I said earlier, your use of time will be pretty much what you want it to be. You may do a lot of complaining, to be sure, but when all is said and done, the values and attitudes that control your thinking will account for many of the day-to-day decisions you make about where and how you will allocate your time and your life. If at this point in your life your job and your career are of paramount importance to you, *and this is the way you want it to be,* then your time control decisions will reflect that importance. Furthermore, it's probably counterproductive—and a waste of time—to complain about those decisions. You have the power and the right to run your own life and make your own decisions. If you don't like the direction in which you are headed, then stop and reassess where you are going and why.

If, on the other hand, you have some personal, off-the-job interests that you wish to fulfill, but your job and career are making severe time demands upon you, then you also have some reassessing to do. You, and only you, can determine what is important in your life. And you owe it to yourself to come to grips with those issues. What does matter to you? Where do the organizational and personal sides of your life meet? Are you kidding yourself about what is really important in your life?

One of the best ways to deal with these questions is to examine your personal time and life line. Because time management is really self management, you need to continually reassess where you are, where you have been, and where you want to be at some point in the future. Once you establish these reference points, you will be in a much stronger position to more proactively manage your day-by-day activities and accountabilities.

Worksheet Five consists of a straight, horizontal line and a series of questions. The line is meant to represent your life. The first thing you need to do when viewing your life in this manner is to mark an "x" at the point on the line that most represents where you are now. The next thing to do is to jot down a series of brief descriptive words and phrases that describe who you are. For instance, I suggest you begin with your age, since that establishes immediately a rough reference point on your line of life. Then, describe yourself in terms that would most readily acquaint a stranger with who you are and what you do. The chances are that the more you write about yourself, the more insight you will develop into yourself and the parts of your life that are most satisfying to you. These "satisfiers" are clues, really, to what you really value in life, and they ought to constitute guidelines as you make future decisions about using your time for those things that really matter.

Next, I suggest you look ahead on your time-life line and establish a point "y," which represents the accomplishment of something significant to you. This "something" could be related to your job, career, education, personal life, family life, or anything of personal significance and importance. When do you want this to happen? What do you want it to be? How would you describe it? What do you want conditions to be when it occurs?

Finally, how do you plan to make this happen? What do you have to accomplish between now and then? What will you have to learn? To do? What steps will you have to take? Yes, how will you have to use your time if you wish to accomplish this "something" of importance?

For instance, I know that six months from the time I write these words, I plan to have this book and accompanying tape finished. If I just sit here and think about it, these things will never happen. Wishing will not make them so. In order for me to bring this manuscript in on time, I have to set objectives, make decisions about how I will use my time, order my priorities accordingly, say "yes" to some activities and "no" to others, give up some things I enjoy doing, and concentrate on a few key activities that will enable me to maximize my use of available time to think and write during the next six months.

Please turn now to Worksheet Five and complete it. I suggest you take repeated "snapshots" of your life using this simple technique. The more you know about where you are and where you want to go, the easier it will be to get there!

COMPLETE WORKSHEET FIVE

My Time Life Line

My Time Life Line

Born

____/____/____

Birth Date

1. Today's date_____
2. Place an "x" at a point on the line that represents where you are now.
3. Describe yourself as you are now. How would you describe who you are to a stranger?
   I am_____

   _____

   _____

   _____

   _____

4. Place a "y" at a point on the line that represents the accomplishment of something significant to you.
5. Describe it. What do you want it to be? What do you want conditions to be like when it occurs?_____

   _____

   _____

   _____

   _____

6. How do you plan to make this happen? What must you accomplish between now and then? What must you do?_____

   _____

   _____

   _____

   _____

Now that you have taken this "snapshot" of your life, I suggest you let this information also serve as part of your agenda for self-improvement. You are gathering information about yourself that will be valuable as you plan and live in a more proactive manner. Most people fail to plan ahead, in their jobs and in their personal lives. They look back only when it is too late and wish they had done a better job managing their time—their most important asset.

TIME DIMENSIONS ON THE JOB

You utilize your time, on and off the job, in a variety of ways. One of the reasons that managing time more effectively is so difficult is because of the confusing configuration of time dimensions—*functions, activities, and roles*—in which you continually find yourself. Mintzberg, in his book *The Nature of Managerial Work,* describes certain managerial activities and roles. According to Mintzberg, you live in a world in which you are responsible for accomplishing an unending flow of *functions,* carried out in an atmosphere of *activities* during which you fulfill a ceaseless variety of roles.[1] To compound the situation, these functions, activities, and roles seldom, if ever, stand alone or are accomplished in orderly sequence. Everything seems to happen at once, and there is no way around it for the responsible, practicing manager.

TIME DIMENSIONS FOR THE MANAGER

Functions of the Manager

Managerial functions, for managers on any level from first line supervisor through president, include some form of the following:

Planning (short-, medium-, and long-range; you set your own time horizons and define your terms)
- Establishing objectives and targets
- Formulating strategies

---

1. Readers interested in more information about managerial positions should consult Mintzberg's *The Nature of Managerial Work,* New York: Harper & Row, 1973.

- Developing schedules
- Establishing budgets
- Anticipating problem situations

Organizing and Staffing
- Developing and modifying the organizational structure, position responsibilities, and individual job design to achieve the objectives
- Obtaining qualified people
- Training, educating, and developing personnel
- Determining standards of performance
- Developing and implementing policies and procedures

Coordinating and Directing
- Implementing plans to carry out the strategies to achieve the objectives
- Delegating—entrusting to others activities, responsibilities, and authority
- Gaining the understanding of others through listening and communicating
- Creating a positive and challenging climate in which people will be motivated.

Controlling
- Measuring progress toward objectives
- Determining variances or deviations from planned performance
- Establishing reasons for the existence of variances
- Planning and implementing corrective action
- Receiving feedback
- Monitoring subsequent performance
- Continually planning and improving

While the amount of time spent on any one of these activities will vary depending upon one's level in an organization and one's scope of responsibility, all managers will fulfill their responsibilities in an atmosphere in which these functions are carried out. Likewise, the manner in which these functions are carried out will vary depending upon the size, complexity, and culture of the organization, and the leadership style of the managers. Nevertheless, these formal and traditional managerial functions will be performed in some manner and to some degree in all organizations, public and private, profit and nonprofit.

Activities of the Manager

These functions are carried out in an atmosphere of activities. These activities include:

- Problem finding
- Problem solving
- Decision making
- Action implementing
- Information gathering
- Weighing, evaluating, and deciding
- Communicating (orally and in writing)
- Initiating and following up
- Appraising and evaluating
- Responding to change

Again, supervisors and managers on all levels perform these activities. The frequency and complexity of performance will vary depending upon the individual's level in the organization, his or her scope of responsibility, and the expectations of the individual. All managers, however, must carry out their functional responsibilities in an atmosphere characterized by highly-charged activity.

Roles of the Manager

At the same time that they are performing activities and carrying out functions, supervisors and managers also spend time fulfilling (sometimes simultaneously) a variety of roles, including those of:

Listener
Explainer
Motivator
Negotiator
Network builder and maintainer
Intelligence gatherer
Information processor
Spokesperson for the unit, project, or department
Originator and initiator of ideas
Doer or operator
Coach and counselor
Arbitrator and umpire
Disciplinarian

Monitor of resources
Continual learner
Change agent

Managers on all levels fulfill these roles, some more often than others and some to a greater degree than others. They slip in and out of these roles as they engage in activities and perform managerial functions.

As I reflect on my scope of responsibility as a manager and my own management of time, I find it useful to view the managerial process as a model having three dimensions: width (functions), breadth (activities), and depth (roles). I have to exist in all three dimensions simultaneously, and my movement in and out of roles, through activities, and into functions is rapid. For instance, I may begin my day in my role as a listener, performing problem-finding and problem-solving activities while engaged in determining why deviations from planned performance (controlling) are occurring. I then may have to quickly slip into the role of initiator and motivator (simultaneously), performing decision-making and action-implementing activities while establishing new objectives and targets (planning).

The point is, managerial activities on every level are carried out in an organizational environment characterized by action and movement, rapid shifting of mental and physical gears, high expectations, and personnel with varying levels of competence and degrees of motivation and stress. These facts of organizational life often have a devastating effect on your "To Do" lists, your daily plans and resolves for more efficient personal time management, and your general desire to develop more effective means of managing your time resource. Just to get through the day becomes an objective in itself, and sometimes it seems insurmountable.

TIME DIMENSIONS OFF THE JOB

Just as your organizational time is characterized by *functions, activities,* and *roles,* so is your personal time. In the personal arena your responsibilities also include a mix of functions carried out in an atmosphere of activities, while we fulfill a variety of roles. Indeed, many people find that managing their time off the job is more confusing and difficult than it is on the job. This is so because many people's lives on the job are characterized by dependency relationships. Responsibilities are outlined for them and they have limited opportunity to proactively plan their functions, activities, and roles. They are told what to do, how to do it, and when to have it done. There are people, of course, who *prefer* to have their sphere of responsibility and activities carefully circumscribed for them. The less ambiguity in their work lives, the better. Others, however, find this condition stressful.

Those who prefer to have their work-related functions, activities, and roles carefully outlined for them sometimes find it difficult to sort out their off-the-job priorities. They sometimes find it difficult to switch from a dependency-oriented, other-directed work day to an expectation of independent, self-directed behavior. It is sometimes difficult to switch gears, and people find themselves frustrated by life's demands. They live with a feeling of aimless wheel-spinning.

Off-the-Job Functions

For purposes of comparison I have organized personal responsibilities into functions, activities, and roles. Functions include:

Planning (short-, medium-, and long-range; you set your own time horizons)
- Determining what you and your family want out of life; setting personal and family priorities
- Establishing time horizons
- Participating in a variety of organizations, hobbies, and leisure-time pursuits
- Determining budgets
- Anticipating problems and conflicts

Organization and staffing, including negotiating and determining who will do what, for whom, and by when

Coordinating and directing, including working with others to accomplish family, church, community, political, fraternal, and other related organizational activities

Controlling, including measuring progress toward desired results and adjusting time and energy in order to accomplish them.

Just as the amount of time spent on managerial functions on the job will vary depending upon organizational level and scope of responsibility, so too will the amount of time spent on these managerial functions in your personal life. Here the variables tend to be oriented not to organizational level and responsibility, but to your personal or family attitudes toward life. Some people prefer a simpler life style than others. Everyone, however, regardless of personal view, does apply these functions to the management of his or her personal life.

Off-the-Job Activities

These functions are carried out in an atmosphere of activities, including:

- Continual communicating
- Problem analysis
- Information gathering
- Problem solving
- Decision making
- Action implementing
- Appraising and evaluating
- Responding to change

As I've said before, everyone's life, while including some mix of the above activities, will contain a different pattern of activity. We all approach life in our own way and order our lives in a certain manner. The activities we choose for ourselves will mirror the patterns for living we have chosen.

Off-the-Job Roles

Finally, in addition to our functions and activities, we find ourselves fulfilling a variety of roles, again sometimes simultaneously. These roles include those of:

Listener
Explainer
Confidant
Coach and counselor
Umpire
Best friend
Lover
Inspirer
Negotiator
Network builder and maintainer
Intelligence gatherer and processor
Mediator
Moderator
Continual learner

Again, each of us fulfills these roles every day, some of us more often than others and some to a greater degree than others. Just as we do on the job, we slip in and out of these roles as we engage in personal activities and perform personally fulfilling functions. Just as our work lives sometimes seem confused, our personal lives also get jumbled and sometimes seem to be a tangled jungle of isolated activities, all leading in indeterminate directions.

HOW ARE YOU DOING NOW?

The next step in managing your time resource more effectively will be to establish benchmarks for your time utilization on and off the job. In order to improve your ability to do anything, whether it be speaking in public, reading faster and with greater understanding, hitting a baseball, or programming a computer, you must first determine how you are doing at the present. You must be able to measure improvement in order to determine progress. To measure improvement, you must establish your position at the beginning. Only then will you be able to set achievable objectives and measure your results.

Later on I will suggest you keep a time log in which you will record the actual time spent in activities and roles as you perform your various managerial functions. The purpose of the log will be twofold:

1. to help you determine how you are using your time now, and
2. to enable you to answer a key question: what relationship (if any) exists between your use of time and the accomplishment of objectives you have established for yourself?

THE TIME MANAGEMENT PROCESS

This key question is, for me, the central issue in time management. My approach may be summarized as follows:

1. You need to continuously establish and fine-tune your objectives
2. You need to determine the action steps that will contribute the most to accomplishing these objectives
3. You need to monitor and track your use of time, just as you would any other resource

4. You need to continuously ask yourself this key question: "What relationship, if any, exists between how I am using my time and my progress toward accomplishing priority objectives I have established for myself?"

Finally, after determining the gaps that exist between your use of time and accomplishment of objectives, you may need to adjust your use of time in order to concentrate on those roles, activities, and functions that will contribute the most to accomplishing the priorities you have established.

I will say more about these individual steps later on; for now, however, we can flow chart them on Figure One, as follows:

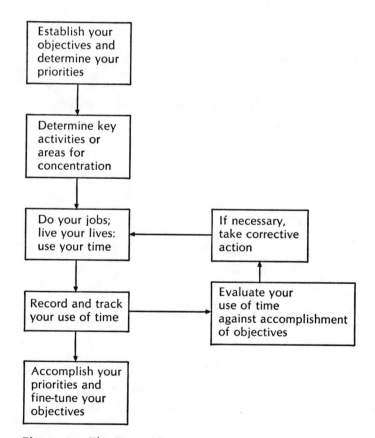

Figure 1.   The Time Management Process

With this process in mind, please turn to Worksheet Six, entitled "On-The-Job Time Usage: A Preliminary Profile." Using your best estimate, indicate the percentage of time you believe you spend during an average month in the indicated categories. Be sure the percentages in each category add up to 100%. And be honest with yourself! There are no "correct" answers.

COMPLETE WORKSHEET SIX

On-the-Job Time Usage: A Preliminary Profile

On-the-Job Time Usage: A Preliminary Profile

This worksheet contains five categories in which we use time. They are: with people, at locations, performing functions, doing activities, and in acting of roles. Please indicate your best estimate of the percentage of time you spend during an average month in each one of these five categories. Be sure the total in each category adds up to 100%.

1. With people   100%
    a. % with subordinates   ____
    b. % with peers inside own
        unit, department, or
        division   ____
    c. % with peers outside
        own unit, department, or
        division   ____
    d. % with immediate
        supervisor or manager   ____
    e. % with other supervisors   ____
    f. % with customers, out-
        side   ____
    g. % with clients, inside   ____
    h. % with general public   ____
    i. % with other (specify)   ____

        _____ ____
        _____ ____
        _____ ____

                    TOTAL   100%

2. At locations   100%
    a. % in own office   ____
    b. % in office of
        subordinate(s)   ____
    c. % in supervisor's or
        manager's office   ____
    d. % in someone else's
        office   ____
    e. % in meetings   ____
    f. % on the road, away
        from office   ____
    g. % other (specify)   ____

        _____ ____
        _____ ____
        _____ ____

                    TOTAL   100%

WORSHEET SIX (continued)

3. Performing functions   100%

   a. Planning
- (1) % in establishing objectives and targets _____
- (2) % in formulating strategies _____
- (3) % in developing schedules _____
- (4) % in establishing budgets _____
- (5) % in anticipating problem situations _____
- (6) % in other (specify) _____
  _____ _____
  _____ _____

   b. Organizing and Staffing
- (1) % in developing and modifying the organizational structure, position responsibilities, and individual job design to achieve the objectives _____
- (2) % in obtaining qualified people _____
- (3) % in training and developing personnel _____
- (4) % in determining standards of performance _____
- (5) % in developing and implementing policies and procedures _____
- (6) % in other (specify)
  _____ _____
  _____ _____

   c. Coordinating and Directing
- (1) % in implementing plans to carry out the strategies to achieve the objectives _____
- (2) % in delegating—entrusting activities, responsibilities, and authority to others _____
- (3) % in listening and communicating—gaining the understanding of others _____
- (4) % in helping to create a positive and challenging environment in which people will be motivated _____
- (5) % in other (specify)
  _____ _____
  _____ _____

   d. Controlling
- (1) % in measuring progress toward objectives _____
- (2) % in determining variances or deviations from planned performance _____
- (3) % in establishing reasons why variances exist _____
- (4) % in planning and implementing corrective action _____
- (5) % in receiving feedback _____

(6) % in monitoring subsequent performance   ——

(7) % in continually planning and improving   ——

(8) % in other (specify)

_____ ——

                 TOTAL   **100%**

4. Doing activities   **100%**
   a. % Finding problems   ——
   b. % Solving problems   ——
   c. % Making decisions   ——
   d. % Implementing action   ——
   e. % Gathering and processing information   ——
   f. % Communicating (orally and in writing)   ——
   g. % Initiating and follow-up   ——
   h. % Appraising and evaluating   ——
   i. % Initiating and responding to change   ——
   j. % Other (specify)

_____ ——

                 TOTAL   **100%**

5. In acting of roles   **100%**
   a. % as a listener   ——
   b. % as an explainer   ——
   c. % as a coach and counselor   ——
   d. % as a negotiator   ——
   e. % as a motivator   ——
   f. % as an arbitrator or umpire   ——
   g. % as a disciplinarian   ——
   h. % as a network builder and maintainer   ——
   i. % as an intelligence gatherer and processor   ——
   j. % as a spokesperson for the unit, project, or department   ——
   k. % as a doer or operator   ——
   l. % as a monitor of resources   ——
   m. % as a continual learner   ——
   n. % as a change agent   ——
   o. % as an other (specify)   ——

_____ ——

                 TOTAL   **100%**

Now that you have completed this worksheet, what did you discover? Were there any surprises? What functions, activities, and roles might you be neglecting? With whom are you spending too much time? Not enough? Where are you spending too much time? Not enough? On what are you spending an excessive amount of time? What are you not doing at all?

Are you spending an inappropriate amount of time performing certain "doing" or "operating" tasks that might best be assigned or delegated to others? Many technically competent managers fall into this trap. It's one of the biggest time consumers of all. They enjoy "doing" certain things and fail to relinquish them as they move into supervision and then up the managerial ladder. The results include too much time spent on the wrong activities; poorly-trained subordinates; and an overall lack of motivation among those who are supposed to be "doing" the activities.

Now, I suggest you perform the same time use and analysis on your off-the-job life. Turn to Worksheet Seven, entitled "Off-The-Job Time Usage: A Preliminary Profile." Using your best estimate, indicate the percentage of time you believe you spend during an average month in the indicated categories. Be sure the percentages in each category add up to 100%. Again, be honest with yourself—it's your life!

COMPLETE WORKSHEET SEVEN

Off-the-Job Time Usage: A Preliminary Profile

Off-the-Job Time Usage: A Preliminary Profile

This worksheet contains five categories in which we use time. They are: With people, At locations, Performing functions, Doing activities, and In acting of roles. Please indicate your best estimate of the percentage of time you spend during an average month in each one of these five categories. Be sure the total in each category adds up to 100%.

1. With people   100%
   a. % with spouse   ____
   b. % with children   ____
   c. % with relatives   ____
   d. % alone   ____
   e. % with neighbors   ____
   f. % with friends from social, fraternal, and religious groups   ____
   g. % with other (specify)

   _____ ____

   _____ ____

            TOTAL   100%

2. At location   100%
   a. % at home   ____
   b. % at vacation or second home   ____
   c. % at office during normal working hours   ____
   d. % at office working extra hours   ____
   e. % in entertainment   ____
   f. % traveling   ____
   g. % with relatives   ____
   h. % in civic, church, or other activities   ____
   i. % other (specify)

   _____ ____

   _____ ____

            TOTAL   100%

WORKSHEET SEVEN (continued)

3. Performing functions and
   doing activities   100%
   a. % working around the
       house   ____
   b. % doing "homework"
       from the office   ____
   c. % moonlighting, on sec-
       ond job, etc.   ____
   d. % being involved in
       community activities   ____
   e. % in social, fraternal,
       and religious activities   ____
   f. % in entertaining others   ____
   g. % in participation in
       sports   ____
   h. % on hobbies   ____
   i. % in just "taking it
       easy"   ____
   j. % in other (specify)   ____
       _____   ____
       _____   ____
                        TOTAL   100%

4. In acting of roles   100%
   a. % as a spouse   ____
   b. % as a parent   ____
   c. % as a grandparent or
       other relative   ____
   d. % as a community
       official   ____
   e. % as a neighbor   ____
   f. % as a friend   ____
   g. % as an officer of so-
       cial, fraternal, or relig-
       ious group   ____
   h. % as a member of or-
       ganization or group   ____
   i. % as a coach or coun-
       selor   ____
   j. % as other (specify)
       _____   ____
       _____   ____
                       TOTAL   100%

As you did with Worksheet Six, review your responses and what you discovered. Were there any surprises? What functions, activities, and roles might you be neglecting? With whom are you spending too much time? Not enough? Where are you spending too much time? Not enough? On what are you spending an excessive amount of time? What are you not doing at all?

As we conclude this chapter, let me point out one of the most prevalent time management concerns of all: the conflict between time spent on the job and time spent with family. This is a concern that affects almost everyone in one way or another. As with most of our time management problems, there are no easy, universal answers. We must all come to a resolution of this problem on our own. All of us must look at our own lives, our objectives, and our priorities. We must communicate with one another, with those most affected by our use to time, with those who share our goals and aspirations. And finally, each of us must say "yes" to some time consumers and "no" to others. The "yes" and "no" answers will be different for each of us, because we all have our own objectives; we all want different things from life. In the final analysis, the important thing is not *what* we choose, but *how* we choose. Do we make our own decisions according to the values, beliefs, and objectives that are important to *us?* Or do we allow other people to make our decisions for us? All of us must deal with this issue in our own way, according to our own circumstances. The answer, however, goes to the heart of our time management problem. The response we give to this issue will help to determine whether we are to be *proactive* or *reactive* in our use of life's most important resource.

Key Points in Chapter Two

1. We tend to project our time management problems onto other people. We blame others or our environment rather than take an objective look at ourselves. We are often the number one cause of our own difficulties.

2. Confronting your own time consumers will help keep you from projecting your time problems onto others and will enable you to be proactive in seeking solutions for them.

3. There are two sides to your time: organizational time (time on the job) and personal time (time off the job). They are often in conflict and each of us must resolve this conflict according to his or her own priorities. There are no universal answers.

4. A time life line is a useful device to use when proactively planning your future. It encourages you to look ahead and establish points of significant accomplishment.

5. You utilize your on- and off-the-job time in a variety of functions, activities, and roles. The managerial process may be viewed as a three-dimensional model with width (functions), breadth (activities) and depth (roles). You exist in all three dimensions simultaneously.

6. Keeping a time log will help you answer the key question in time management: "What relationship (if any) exists between my use of time and the accomplishment of objectives I have established for myself?"

CHAPTER THREE

How Managers Use Their Time

"WHY DO MANAGERS HAVE PROBLEMS?"

One of the first assignments I give new supervisors and managers in my courses on managerial behavior and practice is to go back into their organizations and ask key executives this question: "In your experience, what are the most frequent causes of supervisory problems and difficulty?"

Most everyone enjoys thinking about the characteristics of "successful" supervisors. These can be discussed in a non-threatening and abstract manner, often with little thought given to the realities of day-in, day-out performance on the job. Often, however, general "bull sessions" about successful supervisory behavior result in little real attitude change and even less long-term behavioral change. Motivation to do things differently is often lacking.

Asking people to look at the flip side of the question, and focus on why supervisors experience problems in their organizations seems to be a good way to zero in on specific behaviors and motivate supervisors to examine their own attitudes and prepare for behavioral change. They are invariably surprised with the answers they receive.

THE MISUSE OF TIME— HOW IT RELATES TO MANAGERIAL PROBLEMS

Specifically, almost everyone returns to the course armed with a "laundry list" of answers they have received from their managers and others in the organization. Nearly every list is headed by several reasons directly related to the use or misuse of time. Reasons frequently quoted include:

- "Inability to set priorities and stick to them."
- "Too much time doing other people's work for them."
- "Unable and unwilling to delegate . . . tendency to try to do everything."
- "Not sharing with those supervised what is expected of them."
- "Difficulty in listening and communicating . . . lack of feedback."
- "Lack of realistic objectives . . . poor performance reviews with subordinates . . . people don't know where they stand or what is wanted from them."

Very often these responses help new supervisors and managers set their own agendas for personal growth and development. For those of you who are so inclined, I suggest you take this opportunity to ask your own manager and colleagues the question, "In your experience what are the most frequent causes of supervisory problems and difficulty?" At the same time, and for each response, ask the related question, "With what result?" For instance:

"What are the most frequent causes of supervisory problems and difficulty?"

1. "They keep too much information to themselves and don't share it with their subordinates."
    1a. *With what results?*
        "Those who work for them don't know what to do or when to

do it. They spend too much time trying to read the supervisor's mind and more often than not doing the wrong things at the wrong time."

or

2. "They don't set objectives, much less priorities, for themselves and their people."

   2a. *With what results?*

     "Again, subordinates have to spend time playing a guessing game and often losing. As a result, they often become reactive, doing only what is specifically requested. This, of course, causes the supervisor to criticize them for lack of motivation, which is very unfair."

Now, complete Worksheet Eight.

COMPLETE WORKSHEET EIGHT

What Causes Supervisory Problems?

What Causes Supervisory Problems?

1.

    1a. With What Results?

2.

    2a. With What Results?

3.

    3a. With What Results?

4.

    4a. With What Results?

5.

    5a. With What Results?

6.

    6a. With What Results?

The Ambiguity of Managing Others

Many supervisors and managers begin their managerial careers with little or no understanding of what is expected of them and what their contribution is to be. They are rewarded with a promotion to supervisor or manager because they have excelled as "doers" or individual contributors. The stories are familiar: The star salesman who is promoted to sales manager; the most efficient programmer-analyst who becomes project leader; the engineer or technician who takes over direction of a technical team. Regardless of their backgrounds most of these people have at least one thing in common: They are entering unfamiliar territory, leaving familiar activities and tasks behind and becoming responsible for accomplishing less-than-specific assignments by coordinating the efforts of others, many of whom may be outside their direct chain of command. While the supervisors' activities as "doers" or individual contributors may have been characterized by a degree of certainty and predictability, their managerial assignments are filled with ambiguity.

One of the first things new managers observe is that their time is seldom their own. Unlike before, when they would spend a good deal of time working alone and either being told what to work on or following a familiar routine, supervisory and managerial responsibilities are characterized by continuing interaction with others (within and outside one's direct sphere of control), a lack of routine, and a wide variety of activities, all compressed into brief periods of time! Technical activities no longer take up a large percentage of the managers' time, and technical competency is no longer the fundamental requirement for success. Instead, people-oriented activities, competencies, and skills take up a great deal of time and are increasingly important ingredients for successful managerial performance.[1]

The technically-oriented "doer" or individual contributor can sometimes "shut out the world." Woe be unto the supervisor who approaches managing others in the same way! The manager's time belongs to others in the organization: subordinates, colleagues, and senior managers.[2] The higher up one goes on the managerial ladder, the more important become the cultivation and nurturing of contacts and relationships outside one's own chain of command and sphere of control. More

1. For further analysis of managerial activity, please see Mintzberg's *The Nature of Managerial Work* (New York: Harper, Row, 1973).

2. See Peter F. Drucker's *The Effective Executive* (New York: Harper & Row, 1967) for further comment on this phenomenon.

and more, the effective performance of the supervisor's job requires the obtaining of cooperation and commitment from those in other departments who report directly to other managers and over whom the supervisor has no direct control.[3]

Researchers documenting how time is used in organizational life invariably arrive at a supporting conclusion: that the majority of a manager's time is consumed responding to the needs and demands of others and the requirements of organizational life. Peter Drucker states, "The executive's time tends to belong to everybody else. Everybody can move in on his time and everybody does. There seems to be little any one executive can do about it."[4] Drucker refers to Sune Carlson's 1951 time-use study of top managers in large corporations. The study indicated that most of the time of senior executives is occupied with matters of importance to other people.

Key People in the Organization. Accomplishing results through people, especially through those outside a direct reporting relationship, requires a tremendous amount of time and energy—often more than the new supervisor or manager anticipates. Ambiguities abound, and these result in frustration for the individual more used to accomplishing specific tasks on his or her own, in his or her own way. It is often helpful to stop and examine what is going on, with whom we are relating, and who the people are in our organization who can contribute the most to helping us accomplish the results for which we are responsible. Therefore, let's turn to Worksheet Eight and answer the three questions. They are designed to enable us to focus on who the key people are in our organizations *in terms of our responsibilities.*

COMPLETE WORKSHEET NINE

My Organizational Profile

---

3. Ross A. Webber in his book *Time and Management* (New York: Van Nostrand Reinhold Company, 1972) describes research indicating that managers spend "much time in non-hierarchical relations with lateral and diagonal associates, as much as with subordinates and more than with superiors."

4. Drucker, p. 10.

My Organizational Profile

1. How many people report to you? ____
    List them:

2. How many people do you interact with during a given week or month? (Count those inside and outside the organization, those within your sphere of control—up and down—and those outside your sphere of control.) ____
    List them:

3. Of those identified in question two, how many will contribute most significantly to the accomplishing of the results for which you are responsible? Be objective. Don't kid yourself. ____
    List them:

You will probably discover, if you were honest with yourself, that only from 15–25 percent of those people with whom you interact are, in fact, in a position to contribute significantly to the accomplishment of the results for which you are responsible. This supports our theory of concentration; that is, concentrate and focus your energies on those areas that will give you the greatest amount of payoff. Don't neglect the other areas, but don't expend undue time and energy on them either. The same applies to people. Don't neglect them, but don't spend an inappropriate amount of time on unproductive relationships.

In *Time and Management,* Ross A. Webber compares the use of time of managers on six organizational levels: "general executives" (senior executives and functional area general managers), "sales managers" (regional- and district-level managers), "functional control managers" (middle-level managers), "service managers" (lower-to-middle-level managers of service activities), "operating supervisors" (lower-to-middle-level line managers), and "staff specialists." Webber tallied total time spent by these managers on various activities and compared results. For instance, he found that:

1. Senior executives and functional area general managers spend more time communicating, and with a wider variety of people, than do managers on any other level—and senior executives tend to put in more hours on the job.

2. Middle-level managers and staff specialists move about the organization more. They go outside the chain of command and their communication patterns are the most varied.

3. Lower-to-middle-level managers spend most of their communicating time with those above and below them in the chain of command and relatively little time with those on lateral levels.

4. Service-oriented managers spend much of their time responding to requests, demands, and questions from others.[5]

Looking at management time from another perspective, a recent American Management Association Survey Report, "Executive Time Management," by Dr. Philip Marvin, surveyed the time management practices of 1369 managers ranging from supervisors to chief executive officers. Dr. Marvin's results indicated that, on the average, over half the work-

---

5. Webber, p. 36.

ing day for managers is spent in nonmanaging functions, activities, and roles. The percentages may be summarized in the following matrix:

Percentages of
Time Spent Managing and Not Managing
by Level in the Organization[6]

Level	Managing	Not Managing
Supervisors	39	61
General Managers	44	56
Vice-presidents	49	51
Presidents	60	40

The reason behind this phenomenon is familiar to many managers who have risen from the "operating" ranks. Most managers begin their careers as "doers," or individual contributors. They excel in their technical specialties and are rewarded by being promoted from individual contributor to manager. What then often happens is that newly-minted managers finds themselves to be in a "double bind": having lost touch with their technical specialties, they feel less competent, and are not yet at home with their managerial responsibilities, thus feeling less than competent. The combined result is that, in order to regain and maintain some sense of competency and equilibrium, they often resort to "keeping their hand in" their technical specialty and spending more time than necessary on the more familiar and comfortable "doing" or "non-managing" activities.[7] We referred to this activity trap in Chapter Two. It's well worth recognizing and guarding against, because it's a universal time management problem.

6. Based on data from Dr. Philip Marvin, "Executive Time Management," AMACOM, Division of the American Management Association, 1980, New York.

7. Readers interested in the managing vs. non-managing dichotomy should consult Raymond O. Loen's *Manage More by Doing Less* (New York: McGraw-Hill Book Company, 1971).

Dr. Marvin also concluded that "a manager's day is a sequence of responses" and that the higher one rises in the ranks of the organization, the harder one works and the more hours one invests in the job. Specifically, Dr. Marvin reports hours worked as follows:[8]

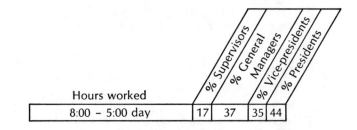

Hours worked	% Supervisors	% General Managers	% Vice-presidents	% Presidents
8:00 – 5:00 day	17	37	35	44

In other words, over twice as many vice-presidents and two-and-one-half times as many presidents reported working an 8:00–5:00 day, as did supervisors. Clearly, the higher one climbs up the managerial ladder, the more pressing the time demands become.

Participants in my time management courses and workshops often begin by assuming that all they need to do to rise above time conflicts and time demands is to ascend the organizational ladder. After completing the course, keeping their own time log, and conferring with senior managers, however, they conclude that effective time management is a skill they must master in order to survive in the organizational environment, succeed in their jobs, and be in control of their own lives.

WHAT THIS MEANS FOR THE MANAGER

Now let's think about the significance of these findings for the practicing supervisor and manager—especially the supervisor or manager who is experiencing responsibility for others for the first time. Moving from "doer" to manager often means traveling a rocky road of hard knocks. The new supervisor quickly learns that getting results through others and making effective use of scarce resources to achieve desired objectives (i.e., managing) is seldom the neat package of functions and activities presented in textbooks. The new manager soon senses that organizations are action-oriented, moving creatures that seem to have lives of

8. Marvin, p. 15.

their own. They are demanding masters, and managers who live with them must continually strike a balance between the needs of their organizations and the needs of their personal lives.

The "conflict" between "human" family and "organizational" family is one of the most difficult conflicts for managers to resolve, and all of us who manage must strike our own balances. Time after time, when I've asked my course participants for their "number one time-management concern," they've responded by describing their "home versus company" conflict. Unfortunately, there are no magic wands to wave over this battleground, and all of us must seek our own answer. The clues to our responses lie, I believe, in our value structures and in what we want for our lives and the lives of those closest to us. Our life objectives must be the parameters within which we structure our decision-making, and each one of us will arrange those parameters in a slightly different way.

One of the important lessons that I've learned about time usage is that we need to be aware of the need for developing interests outside the job. Psychologically speaking, the healthiest managers I've observed are those who deliberately and actively cultivate interests, projects, and commitments outside the organization. As our jobs become increasingly demanding, the energy requirement for managing them increases also. There are times when it seems that we have all we can do to "stay afloat" on the job, let alone have time and energy left for outside interests. Yet it is precisely because of these increased on-the-job demands that we need outside diversions. For our physical and psychological well-being, we require the change of pace and the room to breathe that hobbies and outside interests provide. Later on, when you construct your personal model for "an objective approach to time control," you'll have an opportunity to include some personal time use objectives that I hope will include commitment to outside activities and interests.

THE NEED FOR OBJECTIVES AND PRIORITIES

Life in organizations is often characterized by conflicting expectations, ambiguity, and lack of communication about what is wanted. These inaccurate perceptions cloud relationships with others, consume vast amounts of time and energy, and cause stress both on and off the job. It is because of this environment that a continual monitoring of objectives (both organizationally-related and personal) is a "must" for the manager on every level in any size organization. Objectives are the beacon toward which we are always moving. Without them we become lost and swamped in a sea of conflicting demands. With them we have a visible and tangible guide within which to organize ourselves, use our resources, and plan for the fulfillment of ourselves, our people, and our organizations.

Each and every one of our days is filled with the push and pull of priorities. The setting of priorities is always a tug-of-war. Those who work in organizations soon become familiar with some of the ways in which paperwork priorities are established. Every one of us is acquainted with the "position in the pile" routine, or PIP. PIP is, in turn, broken down into three routines, known as FIFO (first in—first out), LIFO (last in—first out), and FISH (first in—still here). There are times when it is entirely appropriate to set paperwork priorities according to one of the above routines; it is the falling into a routine of one of the above that becomes self-defeating. We need to establish guidelines for managing the "position in the pile" and not being managed by FIFO, LIFO, or FISH.

Another way priorities are ordered in the organization is by the "squeaky wheel" method, or "who yells the loudest." The perceptive manager soon recognizes when this is the method that gets results, and becomes a master at pushing his projects ahead of everyone else's on the basis that they are "absolutely necessary," "vitally important," or "have the boss's okay." Less assertive persons soon discover that their needs, projects, and ideas continually play "second fiddle" to those of their more aggressive colleagues, and the organization develops into a free-wheeling contest for available time and energy resources, with little thought given to organizing these resources around the projects that will contribute most significantly to the accomplishment of objectives.

The priority-setting question, "What does this contribute to our—and to my—objectives?" needs to be asked over and over again. It is a key question for the successful managing of your job, your organization, and your life. Many of us live our lives according to other people's priorities. While some of this is necessary for organizational teamwork, too much of it gets in the way of personal growth. You bear responsibility for making your own decisions about what is and is not important. You usually have structures—your organization and your family—to help you choose, decide, and implement these decisions. Nevertheless, your decisions are, in the final analysis, your own. Asking yourself the above question will help you focus your priorities, your time, and your energy on the tasks and activities that are important to you. The best way to set your priorities each day is according to the contribution their accomplishment will make to the achieving of your objectives.

TIME AND COMMUNICATION

Various research studies document the surprising amount of time that managers spend communicating. Henry Mintzberg, in his article in the July-August 1975 *Harvard Business Review,* "The Manager's Job: Folklore and Fact," refers to two British studies that indicated that the managers involved in the studies spent an average of 66 and 80 percent of their time in oral communication. In Mintzberg's own research study of five American chief executives, the figure was 78 percent.[9]

Ross A. Webber documents research supporting the conclusion that much of the manager's time is "consumed by communications—as much as 60 to 90 percent on verbal communications, perhaps 25 to 50 percent in conferences . . . "[10] With this much time being "spent" on communications, it would seem to be a good use of self-development time to "invest" some of it in honing and fine-tuning your oral and written communication skills. Much time is lost because people do not know how to listen, recognize, and overcome the barriers to understanding, speak well and write effectively.

Listening and communicating effectively with others (by "effectively" I mean gaining understanding) is a problem keenly experienced by technically oriented supervisors and managers. Their preparation for managing has often included little in the way of communication skill building, and their basic orientation has been toward "things," not people. Consequently, when they move from the ranks of "doers" or individual contributors to supervisors, project leaders, or managers, and move from spending 20–25 percent of their time communicating to 70–75 percent of their time speaking, listening, and presenting, they are at a severe

---

9. Henry Mintzberg, *The Nature of Managerial Work* (New York: Harper & Row, 1973).

10. Webber, p. 24.

disadvantage. My suggestion to all readers who must interact with others on a continuing basis is that you invest time in improving your listening, speaking, and writing skills. This investment will pay dividends.

As a final thought before moving on to develop your personal model for improving time usage, control, and management, I suggest that you continually seek not only to clarify the expectations others have of you but that you also help others to clarify the expectations you have of them. Much time is lost and much frustration encountered due to unclear expectations. When people don't know what is expected of them in terms of both their individual contribution and the contributions of their team and department, they resort to guesswork and games.

Unclear expectations lead to the misuse of resources, which in turn leads to frustration and lack of motivation. The more you can clarify expectations and concentrate time and energy on achieving and exceeding expectations, the more fun and fulfilling your job and life will be.

Key Points in Chapter Three

1. Reasons that senior managers frequently cited for supervisory failure often include those related to the use and misuse of the time resource.

2. One of the lessons quickly learned by new managers is that their time is no longer their own; it increasingly "belongs" to others in the organization: subordinates, colleagues, and senior managers. The higher one goes in the organization, the more important becomes the nurturing of relationships outside one's own chain of command.

3. On the average, over half the working day of a manager is spent in non-managing functions, activities, and roles. Most managers begin their careers as "doers" and experience difficulty in changing roles.

4. The higher one goes in management, the more time-consuming the job becomes.

5. The conflict between job or career and family is a universal time management concern. Each of us must deal with this concern in his or her own way. There are no universal answers.

6. Because organizational life is often characterized by conflicting expectations, ambiguity, and lack of clarity about what is wanted, a continual monitoring of objectives is a "must" for the time-conscious manager.

7. Priority-setting is always a tug-of-war. The best way to set priorities is by analyzing what contribution the accomplishment of each task will make to the achieving of your objectives.

8. The majority of the manager's hours are consumed in communication. Perfecting oral and written communication skills will improve time-use effectiveness.

9. Unclear expectations lead to the misuse of time, an increase in frustration, and a lowering of motivation. Time spent in clarifying what is expected and wanted will improve personal and organizational performance.

CHAPTER FOUR

An Objectives Approach to Time Control

A PERSONAL MODEL FOR TIME CONTROL

The purpose of this chapter is to enable you to develop a personal model for your own time control. The model will be useful no matter what your job, position, or role in life is at the moment. As the chapter title indicates, the model is built around the conviction that objectives are the building blocks for effective time management and time control. The clearer the understanding you have of where you are, where you are going, and why you are going there, the easier it will be to focus your time and energy on the activities and processes that will contribute the most to accomplishing the results you want. While it may be true that, "If you don't know where you're going, any road will get you there," it's also true that "any road" will be more frustrating, more costly, and more time-consuming than the "right road," and the "right road" is easier to choose if you have a clear objective in mind.

In this chapter you'll be asked to take a close look at your own situation, your job, your organization, your career, and your life. For the moment, you'll be asked to focus on yourself, for it's *your* time we're talking about and not the "total time" of the unit, department, or organization. The model can be readily applied to a unit, department, or organization, but each of these entities is made up of individuals, and the sum total of their time represents the total time of the organization.

The Purpose of Your Organization

Let's begin. If you are reading this with organizationally-related time control issues in mind, I suggest you write a *brief* (few sentences, one paragraph at the most) statement of the *mission* or *purpose* of your company or organization. For best results, make your mission or purpose statement general in nature and not specific. Think of it as an umbrella under which the statements of mission and purpose of the various departments will fit. Refrain from the tendency to be too general and treat this first step too lightly. For instance, don't begin by writing, "The purpose of the XYZ Company is to make money, more this year than last year." Certainly, the goal of the company is to return a profit, and organizational survival must be the first order of business. However, the return on investment or dollars of profit on the "bottom line" are only indicators of how well the company is doing at performing its basic mission or purpose. Your mission statement should speak to the business the company is in, what it's in business for, and how the company sees itself.

When I ask the managers in my courses and workshops to define their organization's mission, they often respond with wry smiles and quickly grab their pen or pencil. "That's easy," they often mutter, with a know-it-all sideways glance at their neighbor. After giving them several minutes to polish a few sentences, I ask them to compare their statements of mission or purpose with others in the group from the same company. (If the course is being given "in-house" for a specific organization, this is easy.) What invariably happens, especially in an in-house program, is that everyone is amazed at how little agreement there is among mission statements! Imagine—people from the same company who don't even agree on the business the company is in, let alone on why it's in that business and how it views itself!

Here we have the beginning of an interesting situation. The more ambiguity there is in an organization about its basic purpose, the more difficult it will be to establish objectives to implement that purpose. And the more ambiguous the objectives, the more difficult it will be to focus on the activities that will contribute most toward achieving those objectives. Also, the more ambiguous the organizational objectives, the more difficult it will be for individuals in the organization to experience satisfaction in their jobs and be self-motivated when performing these jobs.

Managers and executives who are serious about managing their own time more effectively, and helping others do the same, should invest energy in establishing statements of mission and purpose for their organizations. The more understanding and agreement about purpose at the outset, the easier the rest of the process will become.

Take a moment now and write a statement describing the mission and purpose of your organization.

"The mission and purpose of _____

is: _____

_____

_____

_____.

"The mission and purpose of the _____
                                              (department)

_____
                    (of the ____ company or organization)

is: _____

_____

_____

_____.

Now, in terms of your model, your first two layers look like this:

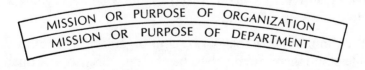

The Objectives of Your Organization

Your next step is to define the objectives of your company or organization. Here is where you should be as specific as possible, in direct contrast to the generality of your corporate organizational mission or purpose. For purposes of my model, I prefer to treat "goal" and "objective'' as synonyms. I realize that some managers use "goals" when referring to "long-term" plans (define your own "terms"—sometimes one year or more) and "objectives" when referring to "short-term" plans, or those to be accomplished in less than one year. For the sake of clarity, however, let's treat them alike and define an objective using the following five criteria. I believe that a worthwhile and well-worded objective must be:

What Is a Well-Worded Objective?

1. clear, specific, and unambiguous
2. expressed within a certain time frame
3. able to be achieved with the resources available
4. measurable
5. expressed in terms of cost.

I realize that some of you are now saying that this is just not practical for you, that you don't know your organization's objectives and that nobody tells you these things anyway. Well, you're probably correct. You may not know much about your organization's objectives, but if so, I suggest that now is the time to learn. And probably no one is going to go out of his way to tell you unless you exhibit some real interest in finding out—so, ask! Talk with your manager, seek out other managers, and read your company's annual report or other literature pertaining to market and financial performance.

Again, please understand that the reason behind doing this is that you will be better able to manage your resources, especially time and energy, in doing your job and helping your organization grow and achieve its objectives. With this attitude in mind, you'll find most managers willing and even eager to brief you on objectives and what the organization hopes to achieve in the future.

Take a few minutes now to describe your organization's objectives as you understand them. Remember, be as clear, specific, and unambiguous as possible. Don't use vague, general terms that will be subject to a variety of interpretations and probable misunderstanding. For instance, avoid such lead-ins as, "Our company's objective is to increase sales significantly during the coming year." What's the problem with this statement? Easy. Everyone will have a different opinion as to what a "significant" sales increase ought to be. Depending upon circumstances, the president might feel that a 20-percent increase is "significant," but the sales manager might feel that, given the resources he has at his disposal, a 20-percent increase is impossible. He might be of the opinion that a 10-percent increase in sales would be significant and a 12-percent one exceptional. Unless this figure is negotiated and a mutual understanding about it agreed upon, the president, sales manager, and company are all headed for trouble.

With the characteristics of a well-worded objective in mind, develop three "short-term" objectives for your company or organization. Let "short term" mean "six months from now," i.e.:

> "By *(specific date—six months from now), (ABC organization)* will have *(state specific result wanted)* at a cost not to exceed *($X)*."

1. By _____, _____
       date   organization
   will have _____
                        specific result wanted
   at a cost not to exceed _____.

2. By _____, _____
       date   organization
   will have _____
                        specific result wanted
   at a cost not to exceed _____.

3. By _____, _____
       date   organization
   will have _____
                        specific result wanted
   at a cost not to exceed _____.

As you develop your objectives, be careful to avoid the tendency to slide into vague, ambiguous generalities. The broad, "mission-type" statements like "to expand," "to increase," "to provide better . . ." etc., are not appropriate as objectives. The more you use them, the more you open yourself up to second-guessing and possibly poor performance reviews later on. Such vague generalities are too broad and ambiguous to be considered measurable objectives. Everyone who hears them will attach his or her own meaning to the words, and it will be difficult to "objectively" measure results and appraise performance.

In addition, always state your objectives in some time frame, such as "by X date," "before the end of X date," or "no later than X date." The time frame should be relevant to you or to your organization's situation, and I suggest the time frame precede the statement of what is to be accomplished.

You will probably find that the most difficult part of developing good objectives will be to express them in terms of cost. It is usually easier to be clear and specific about the result wanted and to focus on a target date for achievement than it is to think in terms of cost. And by cost I mean both *dollar cost,* or budget dollars necessary for the project, and *opportunity cost,* or what the trade-offs will be. Everything you do has its own trade-off or opportunity cost. If you take time to counsel a subordinate, the trade-off or opportunity cost may be less time spent on completing an important project. Yet, counseling that subordinate may be the best use of your time at that particular moment—the "opportunity" you choose to pursue with your available time. If you spend a long weekend painting and papering a room in your home, the trade-off or opportunity cost may be giving up a mini-vacation with your family. The redecoration may be the "opportunity" you choose to pursue at that moment. If you choose to return to college evenings for your M.B.A. degree, the trade-off or opportunity cost may be much less time available to spend with your family. That M.B.A. degree may be very valuable in terms of your career advancement; yet, time spent with young and growing family members may be very valuable in terms of their development. Each of us must constantly wrestle with and decide questions like these. The more effort you invest in thinking through your trade-offs or opportunity costs in terms of personal as well as organizational objectives, the more effective your use of time will be.

In terms of your model, your first three layers should now look like this:

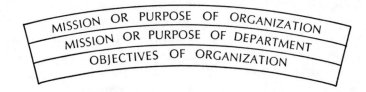

An Example

Let me now develop an example for you, one that will illustrate these first three layers.

For several years I served as Associate Dean for Continuing Management Education at a school of management in Massachusetts. I had operational responsibility for the design, development, presentation, and evaluation of a wide variety of continuing education programs. Their common denominator was that they were all developed for practicing managers.

The school was administered under a well-developed set of mission statements and objectives. The school had a mission, and each program, department, and unit had a mission. The school had a set of common objectives, and each program, department, and unit had its own objectives. Each administrative officer was expected to run his or her programs, department, and unit according to these objectives and within the mission statements. My fellow deans and I negotiated objectives with each of the people on our respective staffs, and everyone's performance was reviewed and evaluated according to how well his or her objectives were achieved.

On my staff were several program directors. Each director was responsible for developing, marketing, managing, and reviewing specific continuing management education courses and programs. Each course and program had its own market and was developed for a specific company or organization (we worked with both profit and nonprofit organizations), group of managers (managers of technical personnel, procurement managers, hospital administrators, etc.), or client system (professional association, municipality, etc.). As an example of what I have been discussing above, I would like to share with you some statements that illustrate what I consider to be an effective way to organize one's time and energy resources around a mission and its objectives. This example can readily be applied to the management of any organization, large or small, profit or nonprofit. I have worked with managers in all kinds of organizations from law enforcement to high technology, and the model we are describing works and encourages more effective performance.

First, the mission statement of the organization can be summarized as follows:

The mission of _____ is to educate men and women for managerial responsibility in a rapidly changing society. Emphasis will be given to the development of applied skills within a sound theoretical and conceptual foundation.

You will note that the mission statement is broad and general, in contrast to specific and focused. It is an umbrella under which all the programatic, departmental, and unit missions will fit.

Second, the mission statement for my department can be summarized as follows:

The mission of _____ is to provide for the managerial community an educational service that will facilitate the development of practicing managers on all levels. We will serve the management education needs of specific categories of managers.

Again, the mission statement is broad and general, but fits neatly with the mission of the organization as a whole.

The third step is to formulate an organizational objective that relates to my area of responsibility. Here we need to be specific, taking care to negotiate an achievable, measurable objective that can be expressed in terms of cost and that relates to the above mission statement. For instance:

By _____, the _____
       date   unit/department
will have increased its enrollment of qualified part-time students in continuing management education programs of fifty or more hours from _____ to _____, at a cost not to
                       number   number
exceed _____ of the total budget allotted for program
              percent
development and marketing.

Here we have a clear and specific objective that is expressed within a time frame, can be measured, is judged to be achievable, and reflects budget reality. There is little room for ambiguity. People charged with responsibility for this program know what is expected of them and should have no quarrel when performance review time rolls around. Time and energy resources can be focused on the key areas for concentration that will contribute to the achievement of this objective.

The Objectives of Your Department

Now, let's continue on to the next layer of objectives, which I call departmental or unit objectives. These should follow the guidelines for a well-worded and workable objective, must be related to the overall organizational objectives and, through them, should be related to the departmental mission and organizational mission.

Your model now looks like this:

A departmental objective that was mine to implement related to the organizational objective of increasing the enrollment of continuing education students in programs of fifty or more hours. The objective also related to the mission of "facilitating the development of practicing managers on all levels," and it dealt with the design of a management education program for new managers of technical personnel. This departmental objective can be summarized as follows:

To complete by _____, the development of a 10-week,
                    date
70-hour management education program for managers with technical backgrounds who have 1–3 years of experience managing other technical and scientific personnel; to enroll at least

_____ participants in the first program; the first group
   number
of participants to begin their program no later than _____;
                                                        date
to enroll at least least _____ participants from the
                          number

following key client organizations _____

_____
list names of organizations

_____;

the above to be accomplished at a cost not to exceed $_____.
dollars

There we have a very clear and specific objective; one that enables us to measure results and would be judged to be achievable with the resources (human and dollar) at our disposal; and it is expressed in terms of dollars or budgeted cost. Naturally, there would be an opportunity cost associated with accomplishing this objective. Because we are focused on this objective, other opportunities would have to take a back seat temporarily. This would be a conscious decision, however, and everyone would understand it. (This is not to say that everyone would agree with it, but that's what managing is all about!)

Now, following the above guidelines, develop three short-term, six-month objectives for your department or unit, i.e.,

"By _____,
specific date—six months from now

_____ will
XYZ department or unit

have _____
describe result wanted

_____

at a cost not to exceed _____."

As you develop these departmental or unit objectives, be sure they mesh with your organizational goals. This may sound obvious, but I'm amazed at how often department heads fail to adequately consider "driving" organizational goals when developing objectives for their departments and units.

1. By _____, _____
    _____ will have _____
    _____
    _____
    at a cost not to exceed _____.

2. By _____, _____
   _____ will have _____
   _____
   _____

   at a cost not to exceed _____.

3. By _____, _____
   _____ will have _____
   _____
   _____

   at a cost not to exceed _____.

Your Personal Objectives

Your next step is to insert in your model some personal objectives. Here is where you look at the other side of the coin, and remember that you are always dealing with personal objectives and goals as well as those that relate to your organization and specific sphere of responsibility.

As you think about your personal aspirations and objectives, I suggest you use the same criteria that you used for developing organizational objectives. In other words, the more specific you can be about what you want to accomplish, the easier it will be to accomplish it. The more accustomed you become to thinking of personal objectives in time frames, the easier it will be to focus your time and energy on them. The more achievable and measurable you make your personal objectives, the easier and more rewarding their accomplishment will be. And, of course, the more you think about the cost (again, remember dollar and opportunity dimensions), the better off you will be economically, and the better you will feel about your personal planning.

Take this opportunity to develop three personal objectives to meet your criteria, i.e.

By _____, I will have _____
      specific date

_____
        describe result wanted

_____

at a cost not to exceed $_____
                                          budget dimension

and/but _____.
                              trade-off or opportunity cost

For instance,

By June of _____ I will have completed my Master of
              year

Business Administration degree at a cost not to exceed $0.00—

my company pays—but I recognize that the time required will

not permit me to get involved with the Community Players (our

local amateur theatre.)

Your personal objectives may be job-related, career-related, or related
to a field of interest entirely outside of your chosen vocation. You may
wish to do something directly related to your job, i.e. complete the
Chartered Life Underwriter study program by X date, if you are a life
insurance agent. You might want to improve your ability to speak in
public (i.e. complete an effective speaking course and hone your newly-
developed skill by teaching part-time in an adult education program) if
you are a manager who will be making an increasing number of public
presentations; or you may become fluent enough in a foreign language
to live abroad for an extended period of time.

Go ahead. Develop three personal objectives that you wish to achieve in
the months ahead. If you get stuck, go back to Worksheet Two in Chapter One and review your change-oriented objectives. They may help.

1. By _____ I will have _____

   _____

   _____

   at a cost not to exceed $_____
   and/but _____

   _____

2. By _____ I will have _____

   _____

   _____

at a cost not to exceed $_____

and/but _____

_____.

3. By _____ I will have _____

_____

_____

at a cost not to exceed $_____

and/but _____

_____.

Your "objectives approach to time control" model now looks like this:

Selecting a High-Return Objective

Your next step is to select a high-return objective (HRO) from the model above. In the "real world" we are always juggling a variety of objectives, and we are constantly struggling with priorities. As I indicated in Chapter Three, I believe that the best way to establish priorities and stay on top of the never-ending juggling act is to continually ask yourself, "What does this contribute to accomplishing my overall organizational and/or personal objectives?" There will be times when you will want to deviate from this pattern, to be sure, but on the whole I believe that using objectives to help yourself monitor and fine-tune your priorities is the best method of time management there is.

So, let's pick an objective to work on. If it's an organizationally-related objective, its accomplishment should contribute significantly to the achievement of unit, departmental, or organizational goals and the fulfillment of mission. If it's a personal objective, its accomplishment should contribute significantly to the fulfillment of some aspect of your personal life. This is not to imply that accomplishing personal objectives does not improve organizational performance. This is obviously not so. Our personal and organizational lives are, for many of us, closely inter-twined. We cannot neatly categorize the events in our lives, as we might do in a workshop or in this book. For the purpose of discussion, how-ever, I suggest you select one high-return objective, the accomplishment of which is of vital importance to you.

Using your model statement, write a high-return objective here:
By _____ _____ will
have _____
_____
at a cost not to exceed $_____
and/but _____.

Your model now should look like this:

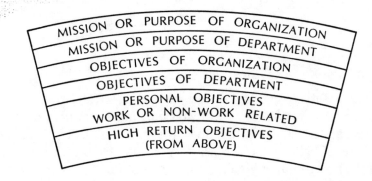

Brainstorming Action Steps — an Example

Your next step is to list the action steps that will be required to accom-plish your objective. The best way to do this is to brainstorm them, or list all the activities you can think of that might be useful in accomplish-ing the results you want. As you brainstorm, don't let premature judg-ment intrude. Keep your "mental foot" off your "mental brake" and list all the activities you can think of. Go for quantity. You'll select quality later. That's the point of the entire exercise!

Depending upon the HRO you select, you may find that some of your action steps are what I call task-related, while others are process-related. Both are important, but it's sometimes the process-related activities that consume the most time—at least, more time than we at first believe.

By task-related activities, I mean those that relate more to measurable results or "ends." You would be accomplishing specific tasks that would, in turn, directly contribute to achieving your objective. By process-related activities, I refer to those that relate more to "means" or less measurable but still important accomplishments. For instance, a task-related activity or action step might refer to the installation of some form of productivity improvement equipment, device, or methodology. A process-related activity might refer to the training necessary to use this equipment or methodology, including resolving the conflict and managing the change required to secure personal cooperation.

With your high-return objective in mind, list all the activities or action steps you can think of that will help you accomplish your objective:

1. _____
2. _____
3. _____
4. _____
5. _____
6. _____

(Is that all? Don't let premature judgment intervene. Your best, most creative ideas lie ahead!)

7. _____
8. _____
9. _____
10. _____

(What are you overlooking? Forgetting? Remember, Murphy's Law exists because we often fail to think through everything we will need to do or plan for when implementing a project.)

11. _____
12. _____

13. _____

14. _____

15. _____

(That's more like it. What innovative, time-saving strategies are suggested by those you have already brainstormed?)

16. _____

17. _____

18. _____

19. _____

20. _____

(O.K. List more if you can, but you've got the idea!)

21. _____

22. _____

23. _____

24. _____

25. _____

(Any more "follow-up" ideas?)

26. _____

27. _____

28. _____

29. _____

30. _____

Selecting Key Areas for Concentration

Following the brainstorming of action steps, it's time to exercise your judgment. You don't have the time to do everything on your list in the most complete manner possible. You don't need to "make the circle too round." Even if you did have the time, doing everything would still not be necessary or advisable, for some of the items you have brainstormed would not contribute that much to the accomplishment of your objective.

You have to select the "critical few" items that must be accomplished well to produce most of the results you want. These become what I call your key areas for concentration, and you must hold yourself—and others—accountable for their accomplishment.

The 80/20 Rule. It is here that you use the "80/20 rule." This is a law of concentration often used in decision making and says, in effect, that in any group of items, the truly significant items will represent only a relatively small number of the total number of items in the group. We see this law in action every day. In any fundraising campaign, 80 percent (or the majority) of the money will come from 20 percent (or minority) of the donors. The numbers don't have to be exactly 80–20; it's the principle that counts: the minority (20–25–30) of items account for the majority (80–75–70) of value.

Other related relationships with which we are familiar include these: in any store, 80 percent of sales will come from 20 percent of the items stocked; in any office or factory, 80 percent of the personnel problems will come from 20 percent of the personnel; in any municipality, 80 percent of the crimes will occur in 20 percent of the precincts. The "80/20 rule" expands into our practice of "key areas for concentration." As far as your list is concerned, 80 percent (or 75–70 percent) of the value will come from 20 percent (or 25–30 percent) of the items on the list. You can't spend an equal amount of time on everything, and some things probably don't need to be done at all. So, get tough with yourself and select 5–7 items (20–30 percent of those you brainstormed) upon which to focus 70–80 percent of your time and energy.

As a continuing example of my model in action, let's brainstorm a list of action steps to accomplish my objective. Remember, my objective is:

To complete by _____ the development of a 10-week,
　　　　　　　　　　date

70-hour management education program for managers with technical backgrounds who have 1–3 years experience managing other technical and scientific personnel; to enroll at least _____
　　　　　　　　　　　　　　　　　　　　　　　　　　　　　　number

participants in the first program; the first group of participants to begin their program no later than _____; to enroll at least
　　　　　　　　　　　　　　　　　　　　date

_____ participants from key client organizations; the
number

above to be accomplished at a cost not to exceed $\underline{\hspace{3cm}}$
and $\underline{\hspace{7cm}}$.
dollar cost

opportunity cost

Here are some (but certainly not all) activities or action steps (in random order) to accomplish that objective. You might have brainstormed them thusly:

1. Study other management education programs and model ours after the most successful, by developing the materials and schedule using other successful programs as models.
2. Select instructors who might be popular.
3. Develop brochure for mass distribution.
4. Call on all the companies that would possibly be interested and leave brochures with their personnel departments.
   (Is that all? Don't let premature judgment intervene. Your best, most creative ideas lie ahead!)
5. Select mouth-watering menu suggestions for the meals.
6. Pick an exotic site for the program and publicize it.
7. Ask instructors to teach material that they know "goes over well."
8. Send monthly mailings describing the program to extensive, popular mailing lists. (What are you overlooking? Forgetting? Remember, Murphy's Law exists because we often fail to think through everything we will need to do or plan for when implementing a project.)
9. Determine criteria by which to select "key client organizations."
10. Select "key client organizations."
11. Hold an open house and invite the business community to come and hear about the program.
12. Organize a special "program preview" for key client organizations, and invite representatives to attend.
13. Introduce instructors to prospective company representatives. (That's more like it. What innovative, time-saving strategies are suggested by those you have already brainstormed?)
14. Determine criteria by which to select representing managers to serve on the Advisory Committee for the program.
15. Select Advisory Committee members and meet with them to discuss program plans.

16. Work with Advisory Committee and conduct a needs assessment: What needs of the managers can best be met by an education program?

17. Ask the president of each key client organization to select managers who can best describe the needs of those to be served by the program.

18. Interview managers suggested by company presidents, and determine needs of participants as they see them.
(O.K. List more if you can but you've got the idea!)

19. Finalize needs assessment.

20. Determine objectives of program based upon oral interviews and needs assessments.

21. Work with instructors to develop material to meet the educational needs described by the Advisory Committee.

22. Working through company presidents, select Steering Committee of representatives of corporate personnel departments.

23. Introduce instructors to representatives of Advisory Committee, Steering Committee, and company presidents.
(Any more "follow-up" ideas?)

24. Determine other key contacts in client organizations—training and development specialists, etc.

25. Secure speaking engagements at professional society meetings, and talk about the program.

26. Make calls on company presidents and key managers and ask for enrollments.
(Good! We've got to ask for the order!)

27. Visit those who are scheduled to participate, and tell them what they can expect from the program.

28. Visit those who have participated and see how they are doing.

29. Design impressive certificates of completion for participants.

30. Determine repeat potential of the program.

Following our earlier suggestions, our task now is to select the "critical few" items we must accomplish well to produce most of the results we want. Here is where we make our "judgment calls" using the "80/20 rule." Of the 30 activities brainstormed, we will get 70–80 percent of our results from 20–30 percent of the items. This means we need to zero in on between six and nine of the action steps and concentrate on doing these well.

Which would you pick? When faced with this kind of objective, people often try to emulate (copy) successful programs already in existence, pick an exotic site, select instructors who are popular, develop attractive brochures for mass distribution, hold open houses, and then call on a wide circle of organizations hoping to generate some enrollments. The net results of such activity are often great disappointment and shattered expectations.

These items are all easy to do but you would, in my opinion, only get 20 percent of your value from them. I would rather pick the following eight action steps, concentrate 80 percent of my time on them, and allocate the remaining 20 percent of my time to action steps of less importance.

My eight "first level" candidates for key areas of concentration are:

1. Objectives 9 and 10 combined.   Determine criteria by which to select "key client organizations," and select them.

2. Objectives 14 and 15 combined.   Determine criteria by which to select representing managers to serve on the Advisory Committee for the program, and select an Advisory Committee.

3. Objective 16.   Work with Advisory Committee and conduct a needs assessment.

4. Objective 17.   Ask the president of each key client organization to select managers who can best describe the needs of those to be served by the program.

5. Objective 18.   Interview managers suggested by company presidents, and determine needs of participants as they see them.

6. Objective 20.   Determine objectives of program based upon oral interviews and needs assessments.

7. Objective 21.   Work with instructors to develop material to meet the educational needs described by those to be served by the program.

8. Objective 26.   Make calls on company presidents and key managers and ask for enrollments.

Not everyone will agree with my choices, I'm sure, but that's not the important issue. What is important is that you develop the mental discipline to focus your time and energy on those relatively few key areas of concentration that you determine will give you the greatest amount of success and payoff on your time and energy invested. The "80/20 rule" still holds: you will derive 80 percent of your value from 20 percent of the items or tasks before you. As you make your decisions about time use priorities, you should ask yourself, "What are the critical few items I must accomplish to produce most of the results I want?" As you manage your time, you must constantly monitor your high-return objectives and focus your efforts on key areas for concentration. The most productive way to determine these key areas is by determining their contribution to the unit, departmental, and organizational objectives for which you are accountable.

Your Completed Model for Personal Time Control

Your completed model for time control now looks like this!

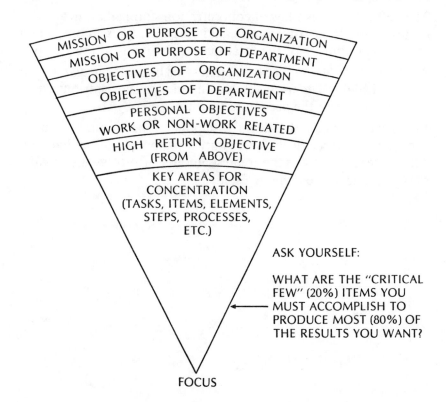

MISSION OR PURPOSE OF ORGANIZATION

MISSION OR PURPOSE OF DEPARTMENT

OBJECTIVES OF ORGANIZATION

OBJECTIVES OF DEPARTMENT

PERSONAL OBJECTIVES
WORK OR NON-WORK RELATED

HIGH RETURN OBJECTIVE
(FROM ABOVE)

KEY AREAS FOR
CONCENTRATION
(TASKS, ITEMS, ELEMENTS,
STEPS, PROCESSES,
ETC.)

ASK YOURSELF:

WHAT ARE THE "CRITICAL
FEW" (20%) ITEMS YOU
MUST ACCOMPLISH TO
PRODUCE MOST (80%) OF
THE RESULTS YOU WANT?

FOCUS

Key Points in Chapter Four

1. A personal model for time control is built around the conviction that objectives are the building blocks for effective time management.

2. Broad, general statements of mission or purpose should precede specific objectives. They are the framework within which objectives are developed.

3. Well-worded objectives should be specific and unambiguous, expressed within a time frame, achievable, measurable, and expressed in terms of cost.

4. Personal objectives should meet the same criteria (above) as organizational objectives.

5. High-return objectives (HROs) should be those that contribute significantly to the achievement of organizational, unit, and/or personal goals.

6. After selecting an HRO, a list of activities or action steps required to accomplish the objective should be brainstormed.

7. The "80/20 rule" is a law of concentration stating that, in any group of items, the truly significant items will represent only a relatively small number of the total number of items in the group.

8. Apply the "80/20 rule" to the action steps brainstormed and select the "critical few" items, tasks, etc. in terms of the contribution they will make to the accomplishment of the objective.

9. You need to develop the mental discipline to focus your time and energy on those relatively few key areas of concentration that you determine will give you the greatest amount of success and payoff on your time and energy invested.

CHAPTER FIVE

The Time Control Log
and Its Significance

THE TIME CONTROL LOG—A TOOL

Except for a clear set of objectives and expectations, the most important tool available to the supervisor or manager who wishes to bring time under control is the *time control log*. There are any number of ways to construct a time control log, and I encourage you to be creative and, after some experimentation, to come up with the method that works for you in your situation and environment. The broad guideline I suggest, however, is to remember the "KIS" principle: "Keep It Simple." This is, in my opinion, still the best rule of thumb. The simpler and easier your time control log is to use, the more you will use it and the more you will get out of it.

I have included my own time control log design with this chapter, and I suggest you begin with this. Modify it to meet your needs, but start here. You will see that I have linked my time control log design to the high-return objectives (HROs) and priority accountabilities I asked you to identify in Chapter Four.

In essence, your time control log should be a simple but systematic recording of:

- what you do
- when you do it
- how long it takes
- with whom you do it
- what it contributes to accomplishing your objective.

It is not enough to record only what you do and when. Doing that gives you some data, to be sure, but you need to convert these data into useful information by examining the contributions that your various activities, tasks, and projects are making to the successful accomplishment of your objectives. This is the most important question in the entire time control process:

Your Key Time Control Question

> "What relationship, if any, exists between the way I use my time and the accomplishment of my key areas for concentration and high-return objectives?"

You need to keep your log—not day-in, day-out, but periodically—in order to gather data about how you consume time. Your purpose is not to pile up random observations but to convert your data into information—and insight—that will enable you to improve your use of the time resource in the future. Without the use of time control log data and your key question above, you scatter your time resources all over the horizon. If you happen to hit your moving objective target, it is probably by accident. By using the data your log provides, and by asking your key question often, you should be able to adjust your sights and take aim on the elusive target represented by your key areas for concentration and high-return objectives.

Many of the studies of managerial work have focused on how senior managers and company presidents use their time. The managers with whom I do most of my work are not seasoned executives but new managers, often with technical backgrounds, who are learning more about managing resources on a day-by-day basis. They don't have the benefit of years of experience as senior executives do, and they often don't have the opportunity to sit down with their senior managerial colleagues to get the help they need in managing their time resource. Managing others in uncertainty and ambiguity is a very stressful experience for many, and the time control log may be a tool to help you bring some order out of what may seem like chaos!

Using the Time Control Log

Worksheet Nine illustrates my *Time Control Log*. You will note that it is designed to enable you to gather the data previously described:

- what you do (the "Event" column)
- when you do it ("Time")
- how long it takes ("Elapsed Time")
- what it contributes to accomplishing your objective ("What did I accomplish?")

You will also note that you are encouraged to examine your log at the end of each day and ask four important questions:

1. Did I use my time to accomplish my objectives?
2. If so, how?
3. If not, why not?
4. What should I do tomorrow to improve my use of time?

Here are suggestions for use of your time control log:

1. *Do* keep your log for several days at a time; *don't* keep it forever. Take your "time temperature" periodically.
2. Record everything you do, initiate, and receive. Yes, this takes time, but it's worth it. You need the information.
3. Don't restrict your log to working hours. What are you doing and accomplishing on your own time?
4. Use your own brand of shorthand when describing events and accomplishments. Write summary statements only.
5. Don't smother your log with details. Be brief.
6. Keep your log as you go along during the day. Don't put it aside and try to complete it from memory. This won't work. Our memories fool us and often tell us what we want to believe.
7. Don't play games with your time and yourself. Your objective is to learn something about yourself and your behavior. Be honest.

8. Be sure you begin each day's log by listing high-return objectives (HROs) you must accomplish. This will help to keep your efforts and energies focused and on the right track.

Go ahead now and complete a log for each of several succeeding days. Use the one included in this book, or design your own if you wish. Be creative. Again, the point is to find something that works for you and enables you to gather data and convert your data into useable information.

At the end of each day examine your log and ask yourself the four questions. You will soon begin to accumulate facts and figures that you will want to analyze. I suggest you analyze your data and convert it into useable information in these ways:

Analyzing Your Data — Broad Trends

First, analyze your data without getting bogged down. Isolate broad trends and try to observe the flow of events that is taking place and affecting you. As you observe events and participate in them, you will have the urge to label some of the events as "problems." Be careful not to label events prematurely.

COMPLETE WORKSHEET TEN

Time Control Log

WORKSHEET TEN

Time Control Log

Day _____ Date _____ High-Return Objectives:

1. _____
2. _____
3. _____

Event (Describe Briefly)	Time	Elapsed Time	With Whom	What did I Accomplish?

At end of day: Did I use my time to accomplish my objectives? If so, how? If not, why not? What should I do tomorrow to improve my use of time?

Resist the tendency to stick labels on occurrences. Think in terms of symptoms of underlying problems. When you observe certain events occurring over and over again, ask yourself, "What's the real problem? Why are these events happening? What is going on here? What can I do about it?"

Managers pride themselves on being problem solvers. Very often, however, they fall prey to trying to solve the wrong problem. They see themselves as activists and "doers," and often jump in with both feet without taking the time to first isolate and define the real problem. They sometimes try to solve symptoms but ignore the underlying problem issues.

It's true that a problem well defined is half solved. It's also true that the most exercise some managers get is jumping to conclusions. It's better to take some time at the beginning to spend wisely in defining the real problem, than to take a lot of time at the end undoing decisions that were made in haste.

Second, focus on time-consuming activities that affect you and over which you have some control. As you review your data and ask your questions, make a list of activities you can dispense with. What are you doing that you don't need to do anymore? What reports can you eliminate? What meetings can you stop scheduling? What phone calls can you stop making? What conversations can you cut short? What are you doing that you should be delegating? To whom should you delegate it? What should you be doing about follow-up and managing rather than doing it all yourself? In what ways might you simplify your job, your tasks, your responsibilities?

We talked about brainstorming in the previous chapter. Use the process again, here. Brainstorm lists of ways to streamline your job. Cut it down to the essentials. Get rid of excess baggage. Don't spend time complaining about the reports you get that you don't need. Do something about stopping them at the source. If it's no longer necessary for you to attend certain meetings, but it has become a habit, negotiate yourself out of them. Be *proactive* and not *reactive*. *It is your time;* you must be responsible for managing it!

Third, examine closely the time-consuming activities that result from existing conditions in your working environment that you might be able to improve, restructure, rearrange, or reschedule. Use brainstorming here, also. List all possible reasons that certain events keep recurring, then go after the most probable ones and try to change them. For instance, you will see that certain events occur with great regularity and require a lot of your time to do the same things over and over again. Don't just complain about "the system." Ask "Why is this happening? Who is involved? What can I do about it? Whom do I have to talk with to change it?"

Is there a "crisis event" that occurs every week or every month? In most organizations there are several of these . . . reports, budgets, meetings, etc. They are time consumers of the worst kind, but most managers learn to live with them by complaining about them. I suggest you don't stop there, because these crisis events are robbing you of your productive time. Find out why they are occurring and what the real problems are. Spend time dealing with the causes and the problems; you may be able to help eliminate time-robbing crises.

Many managers label meetings as "unproductive time wasters." But few do anything about them. Don't spend time labeling and complaining. You only defeat yourself. Spend some time asking, "Why do we keep having these meetings? What are we trying to accomplish? What are our objectives? Are the right people involved? Why are our meetings so unproductive? How could we organize them better? What information do we really need? Why don't I/we/they have the information needed in the form in which it is needed?"

Keep asking questions of your data. The key question is "Why?" "Why are these events happening? Why am I subject to these time loss situations? Why am I not doing anything about them?"

The Time Control Log as Action Plan

Use your *Time Control Log* as an "action plan" for the future. As you log in events, tasks you must accomplish, items you must do, reports you must file, etc., ask yourself, "Do I need to do this immediately? What is the time frame? When is it needed . . . expected? When must it be done? Can it be deferred? Until when? Who should help me do it? Can I delegate it? To whom? Who can do it best? Who has the necessary information, experience, time, etc.? What is its priority?"

As we close this chapter, may I remind you again to keep your key time control question in mind as you review your log, and reflect on what you are learning about your use of the time resource:

> "What relationship, if any, exists between the way I use my time and the accomplishment of my key areas for concentration and high-return objectives?"

As you examine this relationship, ask yourself these questions:

- What is happening?
- Why is it happening?
- What can I do about it?
- What is not happening?
- Why is it not happening?
- What can I do about it?

The proactive manager is the manager who asks these questions and who acts on the answers. This is the essence of time control: to manage time as you would any other resource, with your eyes on your objectives and your mind full of questions. To do less than this is to retreat to a reactive posture and settle for mediocre results.

Key Points in Chapter Five

1. A time log, along with a clear set of expectations and objectives, is a vital time control tool.

2. Your time log should enable you to record:
   - what you do
   - when you do it
   - how long it takes
   - with whom you do it
   - what it contributes to accomplishing your objectives

3. Your key time control question is, "What relationship, if any, exists between the way I use my time and the accomplishment of my key areas for concentration and high-return objectives?

4. The purpose of a time log is not to pile up observations about time use in the present, but to give you insight into improving your use of time in the future.

5. As you keep your daily record of time usage, begin each day by listing high-return objectives you must accomplish. This will help keep your efforts and energies focused on the right targets.

6. Data from your time log should be analyzed in terms of broad trends and underlying problems. Taking time to focus on the real problem often makes for a more time- and cost-effective solution.

7. Your time log can also serve as an "action plan" for the future.

8. The proactive manager: 1. observes how he or she uses time, 2. examines this use against the accomplishment of objectives, 3. asks questions about what is and is not happening, and 4. acts on the answers.

CHAPTER SIX

What Are You Learning, and How Can You Use It?

REVIEWING WHAT YOU'VE DETERMINED

This chapter builds upon the information you gathered from your Time Control Log (TCL) and from asking the key control question. We will examine what your log tells you about your current time consumers and will suggest you reexamine your "All-Time Time Consumers" in light of what you learned from your TCL. There may be discrepancies between what you thought was happening and what is really taking place.

You will be encouraged to look at the time consumers for which you are the primary cause as well as those that are caused primarily by others and by forces in the organizational environment and job structure. I will suggest that you reevaluate your time use on the job, in light of information gleaned from your TCL. Finally, with all this information in mind, you can begin to do some action planning for increasing your time control. You can begin to formulate strategies for needed changes in on- and off-the-job objectives and priorities, time consumers, and time utilizations.

Your Six Top Time Consumers from Worksheet Three

First, reexamine Worksheet Three, "All-Time Time Consumers." Note those that you indicated affected you the most. List the six worst offenders below, in priority order:

1. _____
2. _____
3. _____
4. _____
5. _____
6. _____

Your Six Top Time Consumers from Your Time Control Log

Now review your Time Control Log. Using the information from the TCL, list the six time consumers that your log indicates affect you the most. List these six flagrant time consumers below, in priority order:

1. _____
2. _____
3. _____
4. _____
5. _____
6. _____

Your Real Time Consumers

Compare those actual time consumers from your TCL with those you assumed affected you the most. Is there any overlap? How much overlap is there? What new time consumers popped up? Which ones faded into the background?

Now, as a result of this comparison, list your current "All-Time Time Consumers" below, from most critical to least critical:

1. _____
2. _____
3. _____
4. _____
5. _____
6. _____

Symptoms Versus Problems—Use Your Worksheets

As the next step, consider which of your six "villains" are, in fact, symptoms of underlying problems. For instance, if you indicate that "meetings" are a high-priority time consumer for you, what is the real problem? The chances are that it is not the meetings themselves that are the real problem, but the manner in which the meetings are conducted, with the lack of an agenda, wandering all over the conversational map, etc.

On the other hand, you may indicate that "Lack of Agendas" or "Failure to Follow Agendas" is a high-priority time consumer and that this is not a symptom of any underlying problem but is the problem itself. The point is to use your worksheets as resources and the information they reveal as clues. The problems you unearth will be raw material for your personal action plans.

As a next step, review all your time consumers and reevaluate them in light of new information revealed in your Time Control Log. Where are there discrepancies between what you thought was happening and what your TCL indicated was really going on?

Use Worksheet Eleven, "Analyzing Real Time Consumers" to focus on those that you want to begin working on. Worksheet Eleven is a matrix and asks you to identify time consumers caused by you, by others, and by the organizational environment. It also asks you to think about when these time consumers take place, where, why, how, and with whom—all the information needed for any planned strategy for change.

COMPLETE WORKSHEET ELEVEN
Analyzing Real Time Consumers

Analyzing Real Time Consumers

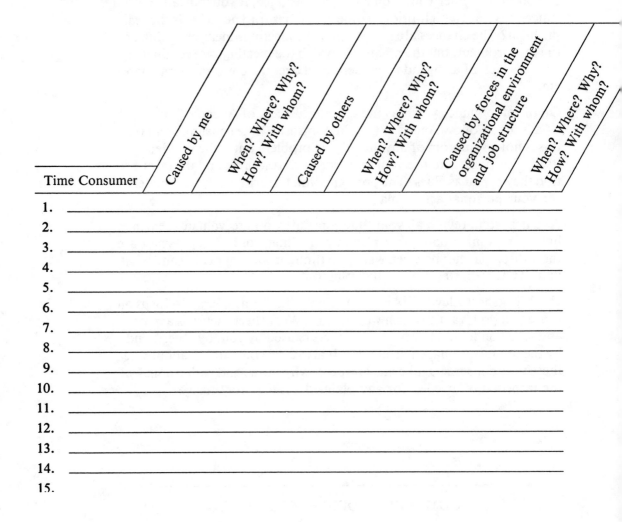

Time Consumer	Caused by me	When? Where? Why? How? With whom?	Caused by others	When? Where? Why? How? With whom?	Caused by forces in the organizational environment and job structure	When? Where? Why? How? With whom?
1.						
2.						
3.						
4.						
5.						
6.						
7.						
8.						
9.						
10.						
11.						
12.						
13.						
14.						
15.						

Beginning the Change Process

Your next task, now that you have useable information about real, bona fide time consumers, is to begin to change and improve upon them. So, from those you identified on Worksheet Eleven, pick out the following:

1. Of those for which you are the primary cause, which offer you the best opportunity for change . . . and why? List them below:

Time Consumer   *Why?*

(a) _____

(b) _____

(c) _____

(d) _____

2. Of those caused primarily by others, which offer you the best potential for negotiation, discussion, and change . . . and why?

Time Consumer   *Why?*

(a) _____

(b) _____

(c) _____

(d) _____

3. Of those caused primarily by forces in the organizational environment or job structure, which might you control, change, redirect, or improve . . . and why?

Time Consumer   *Why?*

(a) _____

(b) _____

(c) _____

(d) _____

Now, turn back to Worksheet Six, "On-The-Job Time Usage: A Preliminary Profile." Using the information contained in your Time Control Log, compare your earlier best estimate of the percentage of time you spend during an average month in each of the five categories (with people, at locations, performing functions, doing activities, and in roles) with actual data as revealed in your TCL. Use Worksheet Twelve to make this comparison.

COMPLETE WORKSHEET TWELVE
On-the-Job Time Usage

On-the-Job Time Usage

	Estimated (See Worksheet Six)	*Actual* (See Time Control Log)

1. With people
   a.   % with subordinates
   b.   % with peers inside own unit, department, or division
   c.   % with peers outside own unit, department, or division
   d.   % with immediate supervisor or manager
   e.   % with other supervisors
   f.   % with customers, outside
   g.   % with clients, inside
   h.   % with general public
   i.   % with other (specify)

   _____

   _____

   _____

   TOTAL   100%   100%

	Estimated (See Worksheet Six)	*Actual* (See Time Control Log)

2. At locations
   a.   % in own office
   b.   % in office of subordinates
   c.   % in supervisor's or manager's office
   d.   % in someone else's office
   e.   % in meetings
   f.   % on the road, away from office
   g.   % in other (specify)

   _____

   _____

   TOTAL   100%   100%

WORKSHEET TWELVE (continued)

	Estimated (See Worksheet Six)	*Actual* (See Time Control Log)

3. Performing functions
   a. Planning
      (1) % in establishing objectives and targets
      (2) % in formulating strategies
      (3) % in developing schedules
      (4) % in establishing budgets
      (5) % in anticipating problem situations
      (6) % in other (specify)

      _____
      _____
      _____

            TOTAL

	Estimated (See Worksheet Six)	*Actual* (See Time Control Log)

   b. Organizing and Staffing
      (1) % in developing and modifying the organizational structure, position, responsibilities, and individual job design to achieve the objective
      (2) % in obtaining qualified people
      (3) % in training and developing personnel
      (4) % in determining standards of performance
      (5) % in developing and implementing policies and procedures
      (6) % in other (specify)

      _____
      _____
      _____

            TOTAL

WORKSHEET TWELVE (continued)

	Estimated (See Worksheet Six)	*Actual* (See Time Control Log)

c. Coordinating and Directing
   (1) % in implementing plans to carry out the strategies to achieve the objectives
   (2) % in delegating—entrusting activities, responsibilities, and authority to others
   (3) % in listening and communicating—gaining the understanding of others
   (4) % in helping to create a positive and challenging environment in which people will be motivated
   (5) % in other (specify)

                    _____

                  _____

              TOTAL

	Estimated (See Worksheet Six)	*Actual* (See Time Control Log)

d. Controlling
   (1) % in measuring progress toward objectives
   (2) % in determining variances or deviations from planned performance
   (3) % in establishing reasons why variances exist
   (4) % in planning and implementing corrective action
   (5) % in receiving feedback
   (6) % in monitoring subsequent performance
   (7) % in continually planning and improving
   (8) % in other (specify)

                  _____

                  _____

              TOTAL   100%   100%

WORKSHEET TWELVE (continued)

	Estimated (See Worksheet Six)	*Actual* (See Time Control Log)

4. Doing activities
   - a. % in problem finding
   - b. % in problem solving
   - c. % in decision making
   - d. % in implementing action
   - e. % in gathering and processing information
   - f. % in communicating (orally and in writing)
   - g. % in initiating and follow-up
   - h. % in appraising and evaluating
   - i. % in initiating and responding to change
   - j. % in other (specify)

   _____

   TOTAL   100%   100%

	Estimated (See Worksheet Six)	*Actual* (See Time Control Log)

5. In acting of roles
   - a. % as a listener
   - b. % as an explainer
   - c. % as a coach and counselor
   - d. % as a negotiator
   - e. % as a motivator
   - f. % as an arbitrator or umpire
   - g. % as a disciplinarian
   - h. % as a network builder and maintainer
   - i. % as an intelligence gatherer and processor
   - h. % as a spokesperson for the unit, project, or department
   - k. % as a doer or operator
   - l. % as a monitor of resources
   - m. % as a continual learner
   - n. % as a change agent
   - o. % as an other (specify)

   _____

   TOTAL   100%   100%

Your final step before developing an action plan based upon findings from your Time Control Log is to run a similar comparison to the one just completed on your time usage off-the-job. To do this, turn back to Worksheet Seven, "Off-The-Job Time Usage: A Preliminary Profile." Using the information contained in your Time Control Log, compare your earlier best estimate of the percentage of time you spend during an average month in each of the five categories (with people, at locations, performing functions, doing activities, and in roles) with the actual data as revealed in your TCL. Use Worksheet Thirteen to make this comparison.

COMPLETE WORKSHEET THIRTEEN

Off-The-Job Time Usage

WORKSHEET THIRTEEN

Off-The-Job Time Usage

	Estimated (See Worksheet Seven)	*Actual* (See Time Control Log)
1. With people		
a. % with spouse		
b. % with children		
c. % with relatives		
d. alone		
e. % with neighbors		
f. % with friends from social, fraternal, and religious groups		
g. % with other (specify)		
_____		
_____		
_____		
TOTAL	100%	100%

	Estimated (See Worksheet Seven)	*Actual* (See Time Control Log)
2. At location		
a. % at home		
b. % at vacation or second home		
c. % at office during normal working hours		
d. % at office working extra hours		
e. % in entertainment		
f. % traveling		
g. % with relatives		
h. % in civic, church, or other (specify)		
_____		
_____		
_____		
TOTAL	100%	100%

WORKSHEET THIRTEEN (continued)

3. Performing functions and
    doing activities
    a.   % in working around the
         house
    b.   % doing "homework" from
         the office
    c.   % moonlighting, on second
         job, etc.
    d.   % in community involvement
    e.   % in social, fraternal, and reli-
         gious activities
    f.   % in entertaining
    g.   % in participation in sports
    h.   % in hobbies
    i.   % just "taking it easy"
    j.   % in other (specify)

         _____
         _____
         _____

              TOTAL   __100%__   __100%__

                              Estimated   *Actual*
                         (See Worksheet Seven)   (See Time Control Log)

4. In acting of roles
    a.   % as a spouse
    b.   % as a parent
    c.   % as a grandparent or other
         relative
    d.   % as a community official
    e.   % as neighbor
    f.   % as friend
    g.   % as officer of social, frater-
         nal, or religious group
    h.   % as member of organization
         or group
    i.   % as coach or counselor
    j.   % as other (specify)

         _____
         _____
         _____

              TOTAL   __100%__   __100%__

What Comparison is Telling You

It's now time to reflect on what these comparisons are telling you about how you are actually using your time vs. the best estimates you made earlier. One of the first reactions to these comparisons will be that there are considerable overlaps in all the categories, both on- and off-the-job. The point is not to get sidetracked with these obvious and natural overlaps, but to reflect on what your actual vs. your estimated time usage is telling you. Are you satisfied with your actual use of time vs. what you had previously estimated? Are there any refinements you wish to make in order to sharpen your focus? If you are not satisfied, what do you need to change? Where do you need to improve? What were the surprises? Who are you neglecting (on- and off-the-job)? Are there any locations where you should be spending more time? What functions and activities need more commitment? What roles need more attention?

Beginning an Action Plan

Your final step will be to generate a personal action plan for increasing time control. You begin formulating plans for needed changes regarding time consumers, on- and off-the-job objectives, high-return objectives, and key areas for concentration. This action plan should be an ongoing project that is continually being maintained, refined, updated, and projected. Review Chapter Five for thought starters. Keep your action plan simple and direct by constantly bearing these questions in mind:

1. What time consumers affect me the most? How do they affect me? Are they symptoms or problems? What control do I have over them? What can I do about them? Who is involved? What might I improve, restructure, rearrange, or reschedule?

———————————————————————————
———————————————————————————
———————————————————————————
———————————————————————————
———————————————————————————
———————————————————————————
———————————————————————————
———————————————————————————

2. What are my high-return objectives? Which will contribute most to the accomplishment of unit, departmental, and organizational objectives? To the achievement of mission and purpose? Which are related to work or career? Which relate to my life and activities off the job? When must these objectives be accomplished? At what cost?

    _____

    _____

    _____

    _____

    _____

    _____

3. How am I going to accomplish my high-return objectives? What activities or action steps will be required? Who will be involved? How will they be involved? Which activities or action steps will contribute most to accomplishment? Which will be key areas for concentration?

    _____

    _____

    _____

    _____

    _____

    _____

4. Finally, what is the most important thing I can do _immediately_ to improve my use of time?

    _____

    _____

    _____

    _____

    _____

    _____

Most of us are aware of the importance of cash flow to the success of our business and family budgeting. We are continually monitoring our source and use of funds. We should do no less for time flow: how and when we use our time, and for what purposes, will count for a great deal of the success and enjoyment we get out of life.

In the next chapter we will move away from the focus on ourselves and will examine some universal time management problems. You will recognize many of them as seriously affecting your use of time. As you read about each one, ask yourself:

1. In what ways does this affect me?
2. What changes need to be made?
3. Who is involved?
4. What objectives should I establish?
5. How should I proceed toward my objectives, and where should I focus my time and energy?

Key Points in Chapter Six

1. You need to examine what your Time Control Log tells you about your time consumers, and compare these findings with your earlier estimates. You may find some surprises!

2. You should think of your time consumers in terms of:
   (1) those for which you are the primary cause
   (2) those caused by others
   (3) those caused by forces in the organizational environment and job structure

3. Some time consumers may be symptoms of more serious underlying problems. You need to dig below the surface and work on the real problems in order for there to be lasting change.

4. You begin the change process by focusing your energies on those time consumers that offer you the best opportunity for negotiation, discussion, redirection, and improvement—and you should be clear about "why."

5. Using information from your Time Control Log, you can also compare actual time spent with people, at locations, performing functions, doing activities, and in roles with your earlier estimates. You may find some surprises here, also!

6. You begin generating your action plans for increasing time control by formulating plans for needed changes regarding time consumers, on- and off-the-job objectives, high-return objectives, and key areas for concentration.

CHAPTER SEVEN

Universal Time
Control Problems

**FIVE MAJOR UNIVERSAL TIME CONTROL PROBLEMS
AND HOW TO DEAL WITH THEM:**

In this chapter we will examine five major, universal time control problems. These are not symptoms. They are real problems and they underlie many of the "all-time time consumers" that we have identified. They include:

1. Differences in expectations; gaps in understanding.
2. Lack of knowledge and understanding of organizational and unit objectives that affect your performance.
3. Difficulty in transmitting understanding through oral and written communication.
4. Difficulty in delegating.
5. Crisis management resulting from a lack of interest in planning.

As you look at these universal time control problems, think about how they affect you and what you can do about them. Go back to the five questions posed at the end of Chapter Six and make notes as you go along. You will add to your agenda for action and will make considerable progress in gaining control of your time resource.

Ambiguous Expectations

In my judgment, the number one universal time control problem affecting new supervisors and managers is a lack of understanding of what is wanted and expected from them. It is very often assumed that everyone "sees" the organization, department, or unit in the same way and that everyone is headed down the same road, toward the same objectives, and with the same time constraints in mind. This is seldom the case. A recent time management workshop that I supervised is a case in point. My group consisted of eighteen new managers, all with technical backgrounds and all working together in a production division technical support function of a large manufacturer. The most senior supervisor had two years of experience managing others. The most junior had been a supervisor only two months. All of them confessed to experiencing real "time binds" on the job, and several indicated that these on-the-job time pressures were beginning to adversely affect their home lives.

Early in the workshop I began to pick up signals indicating that there was considerable ambiguity in the workplace concerning expectations and objectives for these people as supervisors. Not only was there oral disagreement about priority projects, but there was nearly a complete inability to write clear, specific, and unambiguous objectives within any time frame longer than one week.

First privately, and then more openly to one another, the workshop participants began to confess that their days were filled with "fire fighting"—responding to each other's needs for help and reacting to crises. I asked all of them to write their understanding of the mission or purpose of their respective divisions and functions, in addition to their objectives, and there was a surprising amount of disagreement about why their support function existed in the first place. It was no wonder that these new, technically-oriented supervisors were experiencing great difficulty in managing their time resource proactively! Many of them were seeing themselves as failures and, during informal conversations at lunch, over half of them confessed to a desire to quit managing and return to their technical specialties.

The results of this workshop gave me some ammunition with which to approach senior management. Working together, we were able to open up some needed channels of communication through which expectations could be shared and gaps in understanding filled in and smoothed over.

The reasons for the existence of this technical support function were fully explored (management had always assumed that everyone understood), and the contribution that the function was to make to the production process was reviewed. Once the mission and purpose of the function were clear, it didn't take long for the supervisors, in cooperation with their managers and senior management, to develop sets of clear, specific objectives to be accomplished. They worked out individual action plans, indicated key areas for concentration, cross-checked their action plans with one another (good communication did exist and the group had a surprising amount of *esprit de corps*), and were able to become more effective managers of their time resource. During this process their self esteem and motivation increased, as did the morale of their people.

In summary, those managers, with their subordinates, had been in a motivational and productivity tailspin, primarily because of excessive ambiguity in the workplace (remember, they were technically oriented supervisors accustomed to low ambiguity), differences in expectations, and gaps in understanding. These managers weren't sure of what was really wanted and needed, when it was wanted, and who was responsible for it. Left to their own devices, they were making assumptions (mostly wrong) and mismanaging time as well as other resources. Once expectations about the "what, when, and who" were cleared up, these supervisors were able to pull together and do a superb job.

Unclear Objectives

A second, related universal time control problem is a lack of knowledge and understanding of organizational and unit objectives that affect individual performance. The entire thrust of this book is built around the conviction that you cannot manage any resource effectively unless you have a clear understanding of what is expected of you, what your objectives are (with quantity and quality dimensions), and what your key areas for concentration ought to be. If you have all this information, and if you are continually processing it with others in your organization, then you are indeed fortunate. Most people are not so lucky, however, and must first seek out this information, then establish channels of communication to keep informed and, at all times, make it their business to keep the network open with two-way communication flowing.

It's my belief that if you use the model presented in this book and continually monitor your on- and off-the-job objectives, along with maintaining ongoing action plans and focusing on your key areas for concentration, then you have all the raw material necessary to manage your time and energy resources more effectively. There are other elements to be considered, to be sure, but expectations, objectives (work-related and personal), high-return objectives, action plans, and key areas for concentration make up the foundation. An "organization chart" of these elements might look like the one on page 119.

Poor Communication

A third problem involving time control is difficulty in transmitting understanding through oral and written communication. Countless books have been written about the communication process and about writing and speaking more effectively. It would be presumptuous of me to try to summarize some of this writing in this section, for that is not the purpose of this chapter or this book. I do make the observation, however, and you may document it for yourself from data obtained from your time control log, that poor communication skills account for significant time loss in just about every organization. When people don't think and organize well, they don't write well and don't speak well. When their thinking, writing, and speaking skills are faulty, and when mutual understanding is not checked out every step of the way, then time will be misused and mismanaged.

Five key communication difficulties. My experience has convinced me that there are five key difficulties encountered in the communication process:

1. Failure to recognize and deal with the natural barriers to understanding that exist between all people.
2. Poor listening habits.
3. Lack of feedback when communicating, either orally or in writing.
4. Poorly organized oral communications.
5. Awkward written communications.

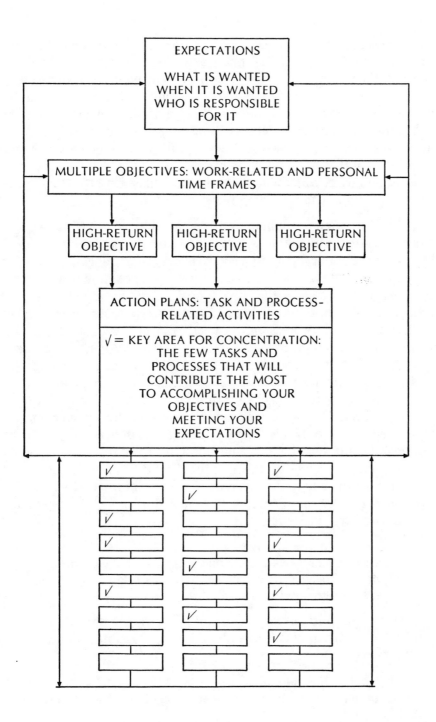

One of the most important elements in gaining understanding through communication (a "key area for concentration") is to anticipate and recognize the natural barriers that exist between people and between groups. These barriers are a complexity of cultural factors, assumptions, prior experiences, attitudes, and prejudices that get in the way of understanding. They exist between all of us, and wishing they weren't there can't make them go away. Neither will ignoring them. Recognize them for what they are, understand that they exist among and between all of us, and work with them, trying to minimize their effects by knowing how subtle but far-reaching their effects are.

These barriers often result in poor listening habits. The feelings we have about the people with whom we are communicating and the assumptions we make about them often get in the way of gaining understanding. As we strive to use time effectively during the communication process, we need to recognize the impact (positive and negative) that our feelings and assumptions will have on the understanding we are creating. It is during this process that we need to check frequently for understanding with the others involved in the discussion. We need to check *what* is understood and be sure that everyone involved understands the situation in as much the same way as possible. Very often, managers and supervisors (like parents) check for this understanding by asking the wrong question: "Do you understand?" This puts the person being questioned in a bind. If this person doesn't really understand, he or she is often reluctant to admit it. Adults don't like to admit to not being sure about something they feel someone else thinks they should know, so they "fib" a little and try to cover up this twinge of insecurity by replying, "Sure, I understand." When they really don't, they often get into trouble with predictable results:

> "But I thought you understood."
> "I did but I didn't really think that was what you wanted."
> "Of course it's what I wanted. That's what I told you."
> "That's not the way I heard it."

Typical, fractured communication. And fractured human relations, too. Both our communications and our human relations will take a lot of time to repair.

How much better it would have been to have taken a little extra time to check for understanding by asking something like, "What is it that we're going to do?'' or ''What is our understanding of the next step?'' or ''Let's share our understanding of how we're going to proceed.'' These are much more ''adult'' questions, and they will help the person or persons involved not to be on the defensive. By checking for understanding in this forthright, non-threatening manner, clear channels of communication will be kept open. People will understand that open communication is expected, wanted, and valued in the organization, and significant amounts of time and energy will be saved.

Another aspect of effective listening relates to the clutter and competition for attention in our everyday environments. There is so much ''noise'' in our surroundings that we sometimes miss the ''music'' and the ''dance.'' In other words, we miss the most important dimensions of an oral communication: the tone of voice, inflection, and nonverbal clues often describing the real meaning of what is being said. There are excellent training materials, books, and films available on the subject of nonverbal communication. Again, our objective in mentioning it is to point out the amount of time that is consumed by misunderstandings. ''Reading'' one another is not that difficult, and the time-conscious person soon learns that it is a skill that will pay dividends. The old adage, ''It's not what you say, but how you say it,'' is still true!

As far as written communications are concerned, I suggest to you the following guidelines for more effective writing. These do not include suggestions about style and composition. The teaching of written communication is not my field. I do, however, feel that following these suggestions will result in more effective use of time when writing:

1. Know as much as possible about your audience. (This applies to oral communication as well.) Who are they? What are their backgrounds? How much do they already know about the subject? What do they want to know? What are their expectations?

2. What are your objectives? What do you wish to accomplish with your written communication? What action do you want? What do you want your audience to do? (These questions also apply to oral communication.)

3. Keep the communication simple. Don't use flowery language. Don't try to impress your audience with ten-dollar words when 25-cent words will do just as well. Overblown words often get in the way of understanding.

4. Put yourself in your audience's shoes. What's in it for them? What benefits? What results? Why should they read your communication, anyway?

5. Decide which form of communication is most appropriate for your objectives: a memo, letter, report, etc. If you want a reply, ask for it. Don't leave your reader guessing.

6. Just as you check for understanding with an oral communication, do so with a written one. Ask someone else to read it and tell you what they think you mean. Don't get hung up on your own "matchless prose." You're not writing for a Pulitzer Prize. You're only trying to convey understanding to someone else, and this can be a very difficult job—so "market test" your writing.

7. Don't be lazy. If obstacles are in the way of understanding, rewrite. I was in a manager's office not long ago, and his secretary brought him a freshly-typed letter he had dictated. "What do you think of it?" he asked "It's okay, I guess," she replied, "but you could be clearer here, here, . . . and here." After quickly scanning the letter, he grabbed for his pen. "I'll sign it and you send it. *I* can understand it." One result for sure: a lot of precious time will be lost in someone's trying to figure out what our friend was trying to say.

Ineffective Delegation

One of the most important strategies for more effective use of time is to fine-tune the art of delegation. Delegation is one of the most difficult managerial skills to execute well. Much time is lost every day due to sloppy delegation. Delegation disturbs us mentally because it requires us to relinquish control, and this is not something that managers like to do. Most successful managers have a high sense of personal responsibility, and this is often nurtured by maintaining close control over that sphere of responsibility. Effective time management through delegation requires that you loosen control over your operation, and encourage other people to "grow" by assigning them jobs to be done and tasks to be accomplished. This is unsettling, because when we assign responsibility to others—even though we may bear ultimate responsibility, for this can never be delegated—part of our reputation as a manager goes with the assignment. It's not that we don't trust our subordinates. We do and we must. It's just that we know that they don't understand situations as we understand them. We can't expect them to. They have not had the benefit of the same experiences, insight, and knowledge. Yet, if we are to survive as managers, we must delegate. And if our subordinates are going to grow in their ability to handle managerial situations, they must receive delegation. They must grow in experience and be tested in real situations. There is no alternative.

There is often a tendency to "do it myself." To some extent this is natural because you are the person who can probably do it best—or at least as well as one of your subordinates. It takes time to delegate, for there is often a lot of communicating, explaining and, yes, checking for that ever-present "must"—understanding. Delegation always consumes more time at the outset, but effective delegation saves time in the end. It frees the manager for the tasks he should be accomplishing and gives subordinates the opportunity to develop. Delegation, in addition to being a prime training strategy, is also one of the best motivators around. People want—and need—self-fulfillment. Most people want to be all they are capable of becoming, and delegation is one of the best ways of "turning people on" to accomplishment.

Guidelines for more effective delegation. Here are some guidelines to follow when delegating:

1. Decide whether or not the job, task, or assignment needs to be done at all. If so, move ahead. If not, scrap it. Don't play at delegating by parceling out worthless assignments. People will see through this soon enough.

2. If you need to, review your people to decide who can do a job most effectively. Who has the advantage, in terms of more time, more skill, more information, more understanding, and more resources? Don't overdelegate to one or more of your people, under the pretext that "when you want something done, give it to a busy person." Resentment will set in and you run the risk of losing those people, because they become frustrated or just plain burn out. Those who don't get the assignments—or at least not the good ones—get frustrated as well. They often leave—if not physically, at least mentally.

3. Be sure your communication is clear. Explain the purpose of the assignment and share your objectives and expectations. Don't

leave your people guessing. Check for understanding. Above all, never assume *anything*.

4. When you delegate and establish expectations and objectives, be sure to set a time frame. Don't be vague, i.e., "When do I need this? Why, I need it as soon as you can get to it." That's demoralizing and unfair. And don't be flippant, i.e., "When do I need this? Why, I need it yesterday." Wise guys often get sabotaged. Level with your people. Be honest. Negotiate priorities if you have to, i.e., "I understand you have several high priority projects under way, but this is critical. Please put aside project X for now and work on this assignment. I need it completed by_____(insert date)."

5. Explain exactly what is wanted and by when. Again, don't leave your people guessing. Check for understanding, i.e., "Now, what is your understanding of this project?" or "Please share with me your understanding of what you're going to be doing." Asking for feedback in this manner allows you to fine-tune the process, i.e., "Sounds good. However, I suggest you also remember that . . . do this . . . investigate such and such, etc."

6. Be sure you as delegator and your delegatee agree on the limits of authority you are granting. Again, don't assume. Share your expectations about when the person is to check back or go ahead. If you expect the person to make all the decisions on his or her own, tell the person so. If you want the person to report back to you "after the fact," let the person know. If, on the other hand, you want your subordinate to check with you at each decision point, explain this also. You'll save time, resentment, and hurt feelings if you take time in the beginning to share the purpose of the assignment, as well as your objectives and expectations.

Inadequate Planning (Resulting in Management by Crisis)

The fifth major time management problem is plain old lack of interest in planning. I'm not talking only about sophisticated long-range strategic planning, or even short-range operational planning. I am talking about day-by-day, week-by-week, and month-by-month planning. Lack of planning results in management by crisis. Every day's a struggle. You fall behind and never catch up. You overload your schedules and don't leave time to accomplish the truly important tasks that always come in at the last minute and are a part of managerial life in all organizations. When you don't think through and write down what you want to talk to key people about on the phone, you end up phoning the same person several times a day when a couple of calls would do. You might drop by colleagues' offices early and often—often without checking to see whether they have time at that moment to give you. You assume that *they* have time because you have time. When they "return the favor," you resent it. A few minutes of thought, the listing of key items you wish to discuss, and the polite, "I need 30 minutes of your time to discuss three very crucial items. Is right now convenient or would 3:00 p.m. be better?" will earn you a friend and his or her attention. It's also a touch of professionalism sorely needed in many organizations.

Planning is a must before you use any resource. You would think long and hard about spending dollars without a business plan. You should think long and hard about spending personal energy—and a part of your life—without a time plan.

Key Points in Chapter Seven

1. Five major universal time control problems include:
   (1) Differences in people's expectations; gaps in understanding.
   (2) Lack of knowledge and understanding of organizational and unit objectives that affect your performance.
   (3) Difficulty in transmitting understanding through oral and written communication.
   (4) Difficulty in delegating.
   (5) Crisis management resulting from a lack of interest in planning.

2. The number one time control problem often experienced by new supervisors and managers is a lack of understanding of what is wanted and expected from them and their unit.

3. A related time control problem is a lack of knowledge and understanding of organizational and unit objectives that affect individual performance.

4. Oral and written communication difficulties often affect time use, on and off the job. Poor communication skills account for significant time loss in just about every organization.

5. Five key communication difficulties are:
   (1) Failure to recognize and deal with the natural barriers to understanding that exists between all people.
   (2) Poor listening habits.
   (3) Lack of feedback when communicating, either orally or in writing.
   (4) Poorly organized oral communications.
   (5) Awkward written communications.

6. Delegation is an important time use strategy and one of the most difficult managerial skills to execute effectively. Much time is lost every day due to sloppy delegation.

7. Lack of planning impedes effective time control, and it results in management by crisis. Day-by-day planning is just as necessary as long-range planning. A time plan, like a business plan, is necessary for the effective use of scarce resources.

CHAPTER EIGHT

Into the Looking Glass

A LOOK IN THE MIRROR

It's time to take a look in the mirror and ask what you're learning about yourself and the ways you're managing—or mismanaging—your time, your career, and your life. No navel-gazing here, and no deeply philosophical look at "Who am I?" Just a few key questions, and a lot of room to roam with the answers.

Pause now and read through the questions on Worksheet Fourteen. Reflect on what you've read so far, the questions you've answered, the worksheets you've completed, and the information you have obtained. You're getting ready to develop your action plan, but first you have to pull together your insights about issues central to your time control and the more effective use of this resource.

I suggest you ask yourself these questions over and over again. Don't stop with the reading of this book. Keep these questions handy and refer to them—and to your responses—often. A copy of Worksheet Fourteen is here for you to complete now.

COMPLETE WORKSHEET FOURTEEN

What am I Learning About Myself?

What am I Learning About Myself?

1. What are my attitudes about time? How does my behavior reflect these attitudes?
   _____
   _____

2. What changes do I want to make in my attitudes and in my behavior?
   _____
   _____

3. What are my priority time control concerns about:
   a. my organizational time, job, and career?
   b. my personal time?
   _____
   _____

4. What am I learning about my organization, my functions, activities, and roles?
   _____
   _____

5. What has my Time Control Log verified? What new insights has it provided?
   _____
   _____

6. What is encouraging about my use of time?
   _____
   _____

7. What is discouraging about my use of time?
   _____
   _____

8. What changes do I want to make?
   _____
   _____

9. By when?
   _____
   _____

THIRTEEN TIME-SAVING STRATEGIES

Before you tie your program together with a personal action plan for time control improvement, it will be worthwhile to review thirteen key time-saving strategies. The effective supervisor, manager, entrepreneur, etc., uses all of these to manage his or her time resource more effectively.

Here they are, a "baker's dozen" with a few words about each one.

Monitor Your Environment and Adjust Your Objectives Accordingly

Your external environment will differ according to your job, function, activity, or role. Regardless, watch that environment carefully. What changes are taking place? With what effects? How will your objectives and responsibilities differ in the future from what they are now? Organizations and families change, and you will be in either a proactive or a reactive posture with regard to these changes. You will develop the habit of looking ahead and anticipating possible effects of these changes on our organization and on you, or you will wait until the changes have occurred and will always be playing "catch-up ball."

Devote Time to Process Issues

As organizations grow, develop, and become more complex, significant blocks of time must be devoted to process-related issues. Most line managers, and many staff people too, are very task oriented—"Let's do it, now!" "Doing it now" is fine. It prevents procrastination and it's a good time control rule of thumb. However, there is a time for impatient action and a time for patient inaction. There is also a time to work through complex humanistic process issues. There process issues are often the "means to the end," and a little time spent on them will often result in much time saved on task issues.

Make Your Meetings Count

Managers spend considerable time in meetings. Numbers and percentages float all around and the only valid number for you is what your time control log tells you that you spend. The average for supervisors and managers probably runs between 40 and 60 percent of an average work week. The amount of time spent in meetings increases as one moves up the managerial ladder, so a few guidelines for running an effective meeting are in order.

By "meeting," I mean any gathering of two or more people called to discuss an issue, make a decision, or take some action. Probably 70 to 80 percent of all meetings in an organization involve a small number of people, and if you're called upon to run a meeting, there are ten "key areas of concentration" to remember and plan for:

1. *Determine why you are meeting and what you want to achieve.* What will be discussed? What are your objectives? Where do you want to wind up?

2. *Using objectives and results as your guideline, outline what is likely to happen during the meeting.* What issues might arise? What conflicts? What information will be needed?

3. *With these issues in mind, determine who should attend.* Who can make needed contributions? Who has access to resources that will be needed by the group? Who has information relevant to the topic and the objectives?

4. *Develop your agenda.* It doesn't have to be a long, involved agenda that is distributed in advance. (It might be, but doesn't have to be.) It does need to be a road map of where you want to go and how you want to get there. Don't overload it, though. Attention spans are not that long. Information overload will get you if you don't watch out!

5. *Circulate your agenda and relevant documents in advance.* Ask people to do their homework and come prepared. Set starting and ending times. Keep the meeting short and tight.

6. *Before you begin the meeting, share your expectations with those attending.* Be sure all people attending know why they are there and what your expectations of them are. Clear up misunderstandings before you turn to detailed discussion.

7. *Stick to your agenda, but don't force it on the group.* Be careful not to stifle discussion. Others may have useful insight into the agenda, and you need to stay flexible—but don't get sidetracked.

8. *Stick to the issues.* Don't get involved with personalities. Keep the discussion focused on the target—the objectives and results wanted.

9. *Summarize what has transpired before you break up.* Also, check for understanding as to who is to do what, with whom, and by when. Don't leave loose ends. Above all, assume nothing.

10. *Circulate meeting minutes and results promptly.* Be sure that everyone understands the issues and the action in the same way. Seek clarity and not ambiguity. And if you want feedback, ask for it!

Simplify Your Tasks

Group like tasks together. Don't try to do everything at once. *Plan.* Cluster your phone calls and make several at once. Pick the time of day most advantageous for what you wish to achieve. For instance, it might not be the best use of time and energy to make a series of phone calls requiring clear decisions and action just before people are likely to be leaving the office at the end of the day. Their minds will be on avoiding traffic jams and not on the issues at hand. True, you may be in firmer "control," but the decisions that others make might not be high quality ones, and the results might leave much to be desired. More time will be spent unscrambling bad decisions than would have been expended if a more favorable time for decisions by phone had been selected.

Also, before you call someone, think through everything you need to discuss with that person. Then tell the person you are calling that you have _____ items to discuss and do they have _____ minutes to spend discussing them with you. Showing concern for their time will pay dividends.

Organize your thoughts before you dictate or draft a written communication. Much time is lost because people fail to plan what they want to say. Memos and letters must be redone. Managerial, secretarial, and word processing time is wasted because of inefficient personal time planning. Personal organization is a habit. Get into that habit!

Eliminate; Ask "Why?"

Eliminate items, tasks, jobs, reports, etc. that you consider unnecessary. Don't "do" them because they've always been "done." Ask "Why?" frequently. It's a powerful word and gets you thinking. Don't continue procedures that are obsolete and out-of-date. Improve. Set target dates and objectives for streamlining such procedures.

Change Work Locations Temporarily

Get away from your usual work place. Work in the conference room, cafeteria, or vacant room down the hall. You're paid for results, not for being glued to your chair! A change of scenery will work wonders and will often help to get you "unstuck." Try not to work near distractions. Don't hesitate to close your door now and again. The "open door policy" is fine but is often only an invitation to kibitz. The open door policy is meant to convey that you're available to help when your people have a legitimate need. What it all too often results in, however, is major time lost due to people wandering in and out. If you need to show that you're available for needed consultation but otherwise don't wish to be disturbed, try using a glass door. They're available and are great time savers!

Trade for Uninterrupted Time

If you need blocks of time to complete a project, report, article, etc., and the phone keeps ringing off the wall, ask a co-worker to "run interference" for you for a while. Shield yourself temporarily from outside demands. Ask someone else to answer your phone, receive unexpected visitors, etc. Trade for uninterrupted time. Your colleague will need some, too, in the near future, and you can return the favor.

Don't cut yourself off from your organization, however. Stay visible. Keep moving. Your people want to know that you are available when they need to communicate with you. They want to know that you know what they are doing and that you appreciate the contribution they are making. You must take the time to keep the communication channels open.

Delegate

Delegate, delegate, delegate. But first determine whether or not the task needs to be done at all, and why. If the task passes the "needs test," then don't overload your best and most trusted people. That's a sure-fire way to burn out people, and you'll wind up with the good people leaving you for less stressful situations, and the people you don't want, staying around. The additional problem will be that those who stay won't be as experienced and competent because you haven't given them much opportunity to grow. Don't get caught in this all-too-common trap.

Use delegation as a strategy for motivation and development, as well as for staying on top of your job. Be sure to set up clear patterns of expectations with those to whom you delegate. These expectations include guidelines regarding:

1. how much authority is granted to each subordinate
2. when they should check back with you or go ahead
3. when the task should be accomplished
4. reporting following completion of the task.

Again, check for understanding, and never assume anything.

Establish Your Objectives, Personal and Job-related

Establish your objectives, long- and short-term, personal as well as job-related. You will almost always be juggling several objectives at once and priority, high-return objectives must be negotiated and established. Brainstorm your action plans or activities that must be performed to accomplish your high-return objectives. Then exercise your judgement and select key areas for concentration, or those activities that will contribute most to the accomplishment of your objectives. Focus your time and energy on these key areas. You'll get 80 percent of your results from 20 percent of your activities. Know your 20 percent!

Begin Now: Take a Step at a Time

Begin now—don't procrastinate. If you can't do it all at once, break the job down into smaller, less overwhelming tasks. Take a step at a time. Set achievable, day-by-day objectives. Do a bit of the job each day. Finish it, then put it aside and move on to something else. Return to it the next day and bite off another piece.

Keep Your Time Control Log; Ask the Key Question Often

Keep your time control log. Analyze the results and compare them with the accomplishment of your objectives. Ask the key time control question often:

> "What relationship, if any, exists between the way I use my time and the accomplishment of my key areas for concentration and high-return objectives?"

Periodic "time temperature checks" will show you how you are using your time resource—and will help keep you focused on accomplishing your objectives.

Plan—Don't Get Trapped in a Round of Low-Return Activities

Plan. Set two or three specific action items to accomplish each day, preferably those that contribute to the achievement of longer-term high-return objectives. Look ahead. Where do you want to be one week from now? One month? One year? Three years? Five years? Organizations plan—so should people.

Don't Be Compulsive—Relax!

Take time to think. Be good to yourself. This will pay dividends.

CHAPTER NINE

Developing Your Action Plan— Tying it All Together

A BRIEF REVIEW

As we prepare to bring our "conversation" to a close, I suggest you return to Chapter One and re-read the sections *Time Management is Priority Management* and *A Four-Step Pattern for Change and Improvement*. It should be obvious by now that self control does play a major role in effective time control. The management of time is truly the management of self. In order for you to exercise self control, you must first *want* to do things differently from the way you are doing them now. As I said in Chapter One, your actions and use of time reflect the attitudes you have about time. In order for us to change the way you manage your time, you must want to change; you must want to alter your behavior. For best long-term results, attitudinal change must precede behavioral change.

Also, in Chapter One I introduced you to a worksheet entitled "Time Changes," (A Four-Step Pattern for Change and Improvement). As you recall, the four steps were to:

1. Decide what it is you wish to change and improve.
2. Focus on the outcome you want, the objective you are going to achieve.

3. Establish the reason(s) you wish to make the change and improvement.

4. Decide upon your target date for completion of the change.

YOUR OBJECTIVE

Your objective in this chapter will be twofold. First, I will introduce you to ten ingredients or elements that should support any action plan for time control change and improvement. Second, we will build upon the four steps above and will create a Time Control Action Plan that you can use in conjunction with the ten supporting elements.

Elements of an Effective Time Control Action Plan

These elements are:

1. The desire to change; dissatisfaction with things as they are.

2. A sense of urgency; the need to get under way.

3. The identification of high-return organizational and personal objectives.

4. The determination of key areas for concentration, the "critical few" tasks, activities, and/or processes that must be accomplished to produce most of the results you want.

5. A tough-minded personal discipline, necessary for the continual concentration of time and energy.

6. Recognition of the twin dimensions of task and process present in all activity, and the need to shift time and energy back and forth between them.

7. A continuing awareness of how you are using your time in the present, and the relationship of time usage to objectives desired and results wanted.

8. The ability to juggle priorities and focus on short-run payoffs while not neglecting long-run opportunities.

9. The desire, willingness, and ability to delegate.

10. The ability—and willingness—to say "no" as well as "yes" to time demands.

Worksheet Fourteen, Your Time Control Action Plan, builds upon the four steps contained in Worksheet Two, Chapter One. Use it in conjunction with the ten elements described above. It's a framework for the more effective focusing of your time resources on high-priority objectives of either an organizational or personal nature. It's also useful as a checklist to remind you of some of the key issues we've discussed and worked on:

- objectives and results wanted
- action items
- key areas for concentration
- time consumers
- key people involved
- task and process dimensions

My suggested Action Plan is shown in Worksheet Fourteen.

CONCLUSION

This Time Control Action Plan brings this workbook to a close. I suggest you use the Action Plan often. Adjust and change it to meet your needs. Come up with a design that works for you.

I've enjoyed our "conversation." I hope you have, too. I believe your time and your health are your two most valuable resources. Neither should be squandered. Use them wisely.

WORKSHEET FOURTEEN

Time Control Action Plan

1. I wish to change and improve:

2. The (outcome) (objective) (result) I want is:

3. The reason(s) I wish to change (is) (are):

4. My target date is:

5. Action items to accomplish my objective are:

6. Key areas for concentration are:

7. Time consumers to avoid are:

8. Key people to be involved are:

9. I will know I have been successful when:

Time Control Action Plan

1. I wish to change and improve:

2. The (outcome) (objective) (result) I want is:

3. The reason(s) I wish to change (is) (are):

4. My target date is:

5. Action items to accomplish my objectives are:

6. Key areas for concentration are:

7. Time consumers to avoid are:

8. Key people to be involved are:

9. I will know I have been successful when:

BIBLIOGRAPHY

Boyd, Bradford B. *Management-Minded Supervision*. New York: McGraw-Hill Book Company, 1968.

Drucker, Peter F. *The Effective Executive*. New York: Harper & Row, Publishers, Inc., 1966.

Engstrom, Ted W., and Mackenzie, R. Alec. *Managing Your Time*. Grand Rapids, MI: Zondervan Publishing House, 1967.

Haimann, Theo, and Hilgert, Raymond L. *Supervision: Concepts and Practices of Management*. Cincinnati: South-Western Publishing Company, 1972.

Lakein, Alan. *How to Get Control of Your Time and Your Life*. New York: Signet, The New American Library, Inc., 1974.

Loen, Raymond O. *Manage More by Doing Less*. New York: McGraw-Hill Book Company, 1971.

Mackenzie, R. Alec. *The Time Trap*. New York: AMACOM, A Division of the American Management Association, Inc., 1972.

Marvin, Philip, *Executive Time Management*. An AMA Survey Report. New York: AMACOM, A Division of the American Management Association, Inc., 1980.

McCay, James T. *The Management of Time*. Englewood Cliffs: Prentice-Hall, Inc., 1959.

Mintzberg, Henry. *The Nature of Managerial Work*. New York: Harper & Row, Publishers, Inc., 1973.

Morris, William, ed. *The American Heritage Dictionary of the English Language*. Boston: American Heritage Publishing Company, Inc., and Houghton Mifflin Publishing Company, 1975.

Ware, James. "A Note on How to Run a Meeting." Boston: Harvard Business School Teaching Note 9–478–003, 1977.

Webber, Ross A. *Time and Management*. New York: Van Nostrand Reinhold Company, 1972.

This is not the end!

Reinforce the techniques you've learned with a cassette tape! Continue to improve your time management skills with authentic verbal examples to clarify the concepts covered in the text. Have the convenience of learning any time—while you're driving to work, cooking dinner, or just relaxing!

Complete the program by ordering your *It's About Time* cassette today!

Yes, I'd like to improve my time management skills with the *It's About Time* audio cassette tape (approximately 90 minutes). Please send me _____ cassette tape(s) at $13.95 each, plus $1.50 for handling.

_____Payment enclosed (We pay postage. Mass. residents add 5% sales tax.)

_____Charge to credit card (We pay postage.)

_____Master Charge _____VISA/BankAmericard _____American Express

Account Number_____

Expiration Date_____

_____Bill me (You pay postage and handling. Authorized purchase order required on orders of $50.00 or more.)

Signature_____
          (Signature required for processing of order.)

All foreign orders add 10% and prepay in U.S. dollars.

CBI Publishing Company, Inc.
51 Sleeper Street
Boston, Massachusetts   02210

(617) 426-2224